# AmericA onWheels

# AmericA onWheels

## TALES AND TRIVIA OF THE AUTOMOBILE

MARK SMITH & NAOMI BLACK

ILLUSTRATIONS BY JAYE ZIMET

WILLIAM MORROW AND COMPANY, INC.    New York

**Library of Congress Cataloging-in-Publication Data**

Smith, Mark, 1957–
America on wheels.

Includes index.
1. Automobiles—United States—Miscellanea.
I. Black, Naomi, 1957–    . II. Title.
TL154.S57    1986        629.2'222'0973        85-31047
ISBN 0-688-05948-1

Printed in the United States of America

First Edition

1 2 3 4 5 6 7 8 9 10

BOOK DESIGN BY JAYE ZIMET

For Clark Smith and David Black
And for Eunice

# Preface

This book is a collection of what we have found to be the most amusing, interesting, and unusual facts, histories, anecdotes, and trivia about the American automobile. In a certain patchwork style, it attempts to capture the great character of the American car, its people and events, and to encapsulate the dynamic atmosphere in which it was invented and developed. If it succeeds in this, then its main goal—to entertain the reader—will have been met. It is not intended as a reference source or a comprehensive history, and it does not lay claim to infallibility. Certainly it is not designed to spur conflict among automotive historians as to exact dates, times, and statistics.

We would like to express our thanks to Arthur S. Eldredge of Peterborough, New Hampshire, who generously allowed the free use of his fine library and whose personal insights gave added depth to the project.

# Contents

## THE CAR

## AUTO HISTORY AND FAMOUS FIRSTS

---

## TRUE LOVE

## UNUSUAL CARS AND GADGETS

## THE AUTHOR AND THE AUTO

# CARS OF THE FUTURE

# YOU AND THE WORLD OF CARS

The Car

# Buick Notes

David Dunbar Buick's first experimental car came to life in 1900.

The company, in its early days, sponsored a famous racing team, whose members—Bob Burman, Gaston Chevrolet, Louis Chevrolet, and Louis Strang—raced Buick Bugs.

Buick's slogan—When Better Automobiles Are Built, Buick Will Build Them—was coined in 1905.

A 1906 Buick won the 1,000-mile free-for-all race at New York's Empire City track.

Buick is credited with the first 4-cylinder engine with sliding transmission; the engine appeared in the 1907 cars.

Buick became part of General Motors in 1908.

The company's first closed car, Model 41, sold for $2,750 when new in 1911.

The one millionth Buick was built in 1923; the second millionth in 1926; the third millionth in 1936. Current domestic sales, as of 1983, are approximately 800,000 a year.

President Franklin D. Roosevelt and Chicago
Mayor Anton Cermak were riding in a Buick
touring car on February 13, 1933, when Giuseppe
Zangara attempted to assassinate the
President.

# Cadillac Notes

In 1902, the Detroit Automobile Company became the
Cadillac Automobile Company. In 1905, the latter
joined with Leland & Faulconer to form the Cadillac
Motor Car Company.

The name Cadillac comes from the seventeenth-
century founder of the city of Detroit, Antoine de la
Mothe Cadillac.

Cadillac is said to have been the first American car to
use a steering wheel rather than a tiller.

Cadillac won, in 1908, the Royal Automobile Club of
London's Dewar trophy—the first American auto
to win—in acknowledgment of the cars' standardization
of parts. For its introduction of electrical starting,
lighting, and ignition devices, Cadillac was again
awarded the Dewar trophy, this time in 1913.

An American pioneer, the company was the first to use
a V-8 engine in the United States, in 1914.

President Hoover used a 16-cylinder Cadillac limousine
throughout most of his administration.

Spare tires concealed in the car body was an American first with the 1933 LaSalle, a car that never gained wide acceptance with the public.

The inaugural parade of 1953 featured President Dwight D. Eisenhower riding in a white Cadillac.

A 1950 Coupe DeVille was the one millionth Cadillac produced; the five millionth, a blue Sedan DeVille, was assembled on June 27, 1973.

When Richard M. Nixon was President, he presented a Fleetwood Eldorado Coupe to Leonid Brezhnev.

## Chevrolet Notes

Louis Chevrolet's first production cars appeared in 1911, but the company itself did not start up until 1913, under the leadership of William C. Durant.

The company's emblem supposedly sprang from William Durant's inspired imagination. His muse appeared in an anonymous hotel's wallpaper.

Chevrolet became a division of General Motors in 1918.

Chevrolet's first commercial success was the 1915 Model 490.

The "Cast Iron Wonder," a 6-cylinder engine, hit the market in 1929 and lasted, in one form or another, until 1953.

The year 1934 saw the production of the 10 millionth Chevrolet car.

Corvette production began in 1953, but the V-8 engine didn't arrive in these automobiles until 1957.

The majority of the first Corvettes were painted white, almost 80 percent.

Chevrolet's 1955 model V-8, which came out a year after the new engines were introduced in the cars, became a favorite in stock-car racing.

Ralph Nader, in his book *Unsafe at Any Speed*, made the Corvair infamous when he cited it as "one of the greatest acts of industrial irresponsibility in the present century."

# Chrysler Notes

January 1924 marked the date of introduction of the first Chrysler.

Chrysler sold 32,000 vehicles in its initial twelve months and established a new record for first-year sales in the industry.

Ralph DePalma broke the stock-car record for climbing Mt. Wilson in 1924; his car was a Chrysler.

The Chrysler was the first American car to enter the Le Mans international car race.

From 1924 to 1928, Chrysler jumped from thirty-second place in industry rankings—the bottom—to third place.

Walter Chrysler bought Dodge in 1928, introducing the Plymouth and DeSoto lines in the same year.

A 1940 Crown Imperial phaeton served as the official New York City parade car until 1960.

The 1956 300B Chrysler broke the world speed record for a passenger car; the Daytona Beach contest resulted in an average speed of just under 140 miles an hour for the Chrysler car.

Chrysler introduced "the Forward Look" in 1957.

The one millionth car was built in 1973.

## Ford Notes

Henry Ford's first car, the Quadricycle, was completed on June 4, 1896.

On July 23, 1903, a 2-cylinder Model A made history; it was on this day that Ford sold his first production car.

---

One of the world's first speed records was established with Henry Ford at the wheel. He reached a speed of 91.37 M.P.H. driving a 999 on iced-over Lake St. Clair in 1904.

George Selden sued Ford for infringement of his patent—for an internal combustion engined auto—in 1903. Six years later the court ruled against Ford, only to be overturned in 1910.

The first Model T was introduced on October 1, 1908; the new Model A premiered on December 2, 1927.

The one millionth Ford car was built on December 10, 1915; the ten-millionth on June 4, 1924; and the twenty-five millionth on January 18, 1937. On April 29, 1959, a Galaxie Town Sedan became the fifty millionth vehicle to roll off the line. The next milestone, the one hundred millionth American-made Ford, followed on November 15, 1977.

A royal blue 1938 Ford V-8 once belonged to President Franklin D. Roosevelt; the car is now housed at the Little White House in Warm Springs, Georgia. Other notable autos are on display at the Henry Ford Museum in Dearborn, Michigan.

The ill-fated Edsel—which Henry Ford did not at first want to be named for his son—met the public on September 4, 1957, only to be dropped on November 19, 1959.

# Hudson Notes

December 28, 1915, marked the issue date for the patent of the first engine built by Hudson.

A 1916 Hudson Super-Six was the first automobile to cross the United States and return; the round trip took 5 days, 3 hours, and 31 minutes from San Francisco to New York, and 5 days, 17 hours, and 32 minutes from New York to San Francisco.

By 1918 the business car had already arrived. One extant photo in American Motors' archives pictures a Hudson limousine with a Dictograph communicating system, automatic heater, courtesy lights, curtains, pillows, foot rests, and a vanity case.

In 1919 the Hudson catalog announced: "Today there is a Hudson Super-Six for each six miles of improved roadway in America."

Evangelist Billy Sunday owned a 1914 Hudson Six-40; other Hudson owners included His Imperial Highness Nashimoto of Japan, with a 1928 Hudson sedan, and Edna Goodrich, "reputed to be the most expensively-gowned actress in motion pictures [in 1917]" reports the American Motors *Family Album*.

The Hudson Motor Car Company commissioned *The Trail of the Arrow*, a movie that starred a Hudson Essex.

Amelia Earhart, in July 1932, christened Hudson's new Essex Terraplane series of cars.

The ashtray became a standard item in 1937.

Hudson's Hornet, which became a favorite stock-car racer, was introduced in 1951.

The last Hudson was built in 1957.

## Lincoln Notes

The Lincoln was named after—who else?—President Abraham Lincoln.

Henry Leland's first Lincoln left the factory in April 1920.

In 1922, Henry Ford took over the company for $8 million.

Edsel Ford, who became president of the Lincoln Motor Company after the Lelands left in 1923, selected the greyhound mascot, which was produced by Gorham.

Four-wheel brakes were introduced in the production cars in 1927.

The Lincoln Continental's first year was 1940; the year before, it was called the Lincoln-Zephyr. During the war years, production of the Continental was stopped; the car returned to the market—in updated form— in 1956.

The first Lincoln Continental to be offered to a customer was numbered 3, and its license plate had Jackie Cooper's name on it; it eventually ended up with Mickey Rooney.

The 1970 Mark III was the first American car to offer steel-belted radial tires as standard equipment.

The 1983 statistics for domestic passenger car sales for Lincoln tally to 101,574 vehicles.

Modern Lincolns now boast an information center that lets the driver know his average speed, average miles per gallon, estimated time of arrival at destination, and much more.

## Nash Notes

The first Nash auto hit the roads in late 1917.

Nash introduced a timely auto accessory in 1924: the electric clock.

In honor of the President-elect's wife, Nash in 1933 offered a color dubbed "Eleanor Blue."

---

The company's one millionth car rolled off the line in 1934.

Single-unit or "unitized" auto body construction began in 1941 with the introduction of the Nash 600.

The 1948 Mount Washington hill climb produced a new record, which E. G. "Cannonball" Baker set in a Nash 600 Sedan.

The first seat belts in an American car were introduced in the 1950 Statesman and Ambassador models of the Nash line.

Claimed to be the first compact car, the Nash Rambler was offered to the public in 1950.

Nash-Kelvinator Corp. merged with the Hudson Motor Car Co. on May 1, 1954, to become the American Motors Corp.

The last Nash produced was in 1957.

# Oldsmobile Notes

The first Oldsmobile was built in 1897, when the Olds Motor Vehicle Company was incorporated.

The original curved dash runabout appeared in 1899 and sold for approximately $650.

---

In 1901, approximately 425 Oldsmobiles were built; in 1905, when "In My Merry Oldsmobile" was written, the company produced about 6,500 vehicles.

An Oldsmobile auto, the Pirate, ran 5 miles in 6½ minutes to break the world's speed record in 1903.

In 1905, Oldsmobile's Old Scout crossed the country in 44 days during the first transcontinental race, which had been staged by the company.

In the late 1900s, William Durant, the founder of General Motors, tried to buy Ford. Ford wanted $3 million dollars in 1908 for his business; Durant was willing to give him stock but not cash, and the deal was never made.

The 1923 Model 30, a 6-cylinder car that sold for $750, crossed the country in twelve and a half days with its transmission locked in high gear. Cannonball Baker made the New York-to-Los Angeles trip.

Full automatic transmission appeared in 1939.

Phil Hall, in a 1982 edition of Old Cars, wrote: "If you had to pick one car that started the post World War II horsepower race, it would be the 1949 Oldsmobile 88."

The 1983 figure for domestic passenger car sales for the Oldsmobile division of General Motors is 1,007,559.

# Packard Notes

The first Packard car came out on November 6, 1899, in Warren, Ohio.

The Packard badge included a representation of a pelican and the arms of the Packers of Baddow, Essex, in England.

A Packard, the Old Pacific, driven by Tom Fetch of Jefferson, Ohio, was the second car to cross the country, in 1903. Marius Krarup of New York was his passenger.

In 1914, Packard invented the spiral bevel gear.

Ralph DePalma established the world's mile record in 1919 in a Packard 905. His speed was 149.8 M.P.H.

Herbert Hoover's first automobile was a Packard.

Orders, in 1922, were coming into the factory so quickly that the employees voluntarily gave up or delayed their vacations to get the cars out.

In 1923, a Packard became the first car in America to use four wheel brakes.

Prince Bibesco of Romania "conquered" the Sahara Desert in a Packard.

Packards had a place in the White House garage for many years, during Harding's, Hoover's, Franklin Roosevelt's, and Truman's administrations.

## Pierce-Arrow Notes

The first Motorette was built in 1901 and sold for $850.

In 1902, Pierce-Arrow Motorettes won blue ribbons for the Automobile Club of America (ACA) endurance run and the Long Island Auto Club endurance run. A touring model won a gold medal in the New York-to-Pittsburgh endurance run in 1903.

Pierce-Arrow's winning streak continued in 1904, when the company's cars won the Mount Washington Hill Climb and the Grand Prize at the Louisiana Purchase Exposition.

The Glidden Tour winners for the years 1905, 1906, 1907, 1908, and 1909 were Pierce-Arrows.

The Model 66 Pierce-Arrow was the largest production car in the United States until 1917.

A Pierce-Arrow brought President Calvin Coolidge and president-elect Herbert Hoover to the inauguration ceremony in 1929.

All five automobiles of Coolidge's administration were Pierce-Arrows.

The company developed a V-12 motor in 1931.

In 1933, a Pierce-Arrow topped 14 world records in a single day at Salduro, Utah.

Pierce-Arrow's last year of operation was 1937.

## Plymouth Notes

Plymouth's emblem derives from early American roots; it is a depiction of the pilgrim ship the *Mayflower*.

Chrysler introduced the Plymouth line in 1928.

The 39th National Automobile Show displayed an innovative vacuum-powered convertible top on a Plymouth.

The Suburban, a steel station wagon, came out in 1949.

*Old Cars* reported in the early eighties that Plymouth's "Plain Jane" business coupes of 1949–52, which are rarely seen at car shows, are becoming collectibles in their own right.

A Chrysler Corp. gas-turbine engine was installed and passed its tests in a Plymouth car.

The company produced its ten millionth car in 1957.

Plymouth's sporty answer to the Corvair Monza and the Mustang—the Barracuda—arrived on the scene in May 1964.

Leon Mandel, noted auto historian and author of *American Cars*, calls the Road Runner (1968) "perhaps the ultimate street ripper of them all," which eventually became "the darling of the street racers."

In 1983, total domestic passenger car sales for the Plymouth division of Chrysler Corp. came to 265,608 vehicles.

## Pontiac Notes

The first Pontiac was introduced on January 9, 1926, at the New York Automobile Show.

Pontiac's original Indian emblem was a representation of the chief of the same name, the leader of the Ottawa Indians, who was known for his intelligence as a strategist and tactician.

The one millionth car rolled out of the factory in 1935, the fourteen millionth in 1970.

The 1954 Pontiac was touted as "General Motor's Masterpiece."

Pontiac shrugged off its stodgy reputation in the fifties, when it became known for its race cars and racy options on its passenger cars. This was the era of Semon Knudsen, Pete Estes, and John DeLorean.

The GTO's introduction was greeted with a song called "Little GTO," recorded by Ronnie and the Daytonas, and a promotional campaign that included T-shirts, shoes, and more. The car's nickname was the Goat.

The 1964 Tempest is credited as being the first of the Muscle Cars.

*The Smothers Brothers Comedy Hour* was sponsored by Pontiac.

Burt Reynolds appeared in the company's sales catalog in 1981, publicizing the limited production run of Trans Am "Bandit" replicas of the movie star's car in *Smokey and the Bandit*.

Pontiac's domestic passenger car sales for 1983 totaled 553,135.

## Rambler Notes

The first experimental Rambler, built in 1897, preceded the first offered for sale by five years.

President Theodore Roosevelt rode in a 1905 Surrey Type Two Rambler in a parade in Louisville, Kentucky, on April 4, 1905.

In 1908, a Rambler functioned as a pursuit car when its owner chased and captured a horse thief. The chase—from Kankakee, Illinois, to Rensselaer, Indiana—lasted 13 hours.

American Motors archives note that a 1910 Model 55 Rambler was traded for six cows—not the usual price for the automobile!

The Rambler name was revived in 1950 as a Nash car.

The first American headrests appeared as options in the Rambler Six, Rebel V-8, and Ambassador lines of American Motors.

Winner of the 1960 Mobilgas Economy Run, an automatic Rambler American came in with 28.35 miles per gallon. It won again in 1962 and 1963.

The company's ad campaign in 1965 boasted of "sensible spectaculars."

The two millionth "new" Rambler was built on February 1, 1962.

The last Rambler rolled off the line on June 30, 1969.

# Rolls-Royce Notes

The Rolls-Royce of America, Inc. company of Springfield, Massachusetts, produced the classic cars from January 17, 1921, to 1931 (although some auto historians maintain that the last ones sold were in 1935).

The Silver Ghost had a 6-cylinder engine and a 143½-inch wheelbase.

Production of the Springfield cars is estimated at approximately 3,000—Phantoms and Silver Ghosts combined.

Twelve different body designs were offered in the Springfield catalog.

The Rolls-Royce figurehead—the Spirit of Ecstasy by Charles Sykes—was selected for the grand cars in 1911. The mascot won the top prize at the *Concours des Bouchons des Radiateurs* in Paris, France.

Rolls-Royce of America, Inc. acquired Brewster in late 1925. Brewster had already been providing many of the body designs for the cars.

For the first two years of American production, Rolls-Royces were supervised by British workmen.

---

More left-hand-drive cars were built in 1925 than in any year previously; after that, left-hand-drive cars predominated.

In 1926, the Phantom I had its American debut.

Irving Berlin was a Rolls-Royce fan; he walked into a New York dealership and after browsing for a while, nonchalantly wrote out a check for his new Salamanca Permanent, which was to be delivered the next day.

---

# Price List of March 1, 1924— Rolls-Royce of America, Inc.

## ROLLS-ROYCE CHASSIS COMPLETE INCLUDING ROLLS-ROYCE CUSTOM COACH WORK

THE OPEN MOTOR
CARRIAGES

The "Pall Mall" . . . . . $10,900
4 and 5 passenger Phaeton

The "Picadilly" . . . . . $11,400
2 and 3 passenger Roadster

The "Oxford" . . . . . . . $11,450
6 and 7 passenger Touring

THE ENCLOSED MOTOR
CARRIAGES

The "Tilbury" . . . . . . . $12,800
Enclosed Drive Limousine, Permanent or Collapsible

The "Windsor" . . . . . $12,850
Open Drive Limousine

The "Pickwick" . . . . . $12,900
7 passenger Sedan

The "Canterbury" . . $12,900
Suburban Limousine

THE FORMAL MOTOR
CARRIAGES

The "Arlington" . . . . $13,050
Limousine Brougham

The "Salamanca" . . . $13,500
Collapsible Cabriolet

---

THE CAR

The "Riviera"....... $13,500
Permanent ¾ Cabriolet, 15"
side quarter windows

The "Mayfair" ...... $13,800
Permanent Full Cabriolet

## REGULAR EXTRA EQUIPMENT

Trunk Rack, Front Bumper, Black (Allen) Radiator Shutter, and Built-in Rear Shock Absorbers, all attached at Works, $150.00.

F.O.B. Springfield, Mass.

## EXTRA EQUIPMENT AT EXTRA CHARGE
### All Prices subject to change without Notice

| | |
|---|---|
| Trunk Rack | $90.00 |
| Trunk fitted with 3 suitcases | $125.00 |
| Heater | $75.00 |
| Stop Signal Light (Rolls-Royce design) | $30.00 |
| Front Bumper | $25.00 |
| Rear Bumper | $35.00 |
| Radiator Shutter (Black) | $20.00 |
| Radiator Shutter (Nic. Sil.) | $40.00 |
| Rear Shock Absorbers | $67.50 |
| J-H Tonneau Windshield (Nic. Plated Detachable) | $185.00 |
| Spring Gaiters (set of 4 Menard) | $30.00 |
| Tire Cover (tire only) | $10.00 |
| Tire Cover (entire wheel) | $15.00 |
| Fire Extinguisher (Pyrene Nic. Finish) | $12.50 |
| Chains (Weed) | $9.00 |
| Mirrorscope (attached to tire) | $30.00 |
| Mirrorscope (attached to W/S) | $20.00 |
| Lucas Dimmer Switch | $17.50 |
| Windshield Wiper—Automatic | $20.00 |
| Searchlight—no Mirror | $18.50 |
| Searchlight—with Mirror | $20.00 |
| English Leather Upholstery (Open Cars) | $150.00 |
| English Leather Upholstery (Closed Cars) | $250.00 |
| Pull Up Straps—per set | $15.00 |
| Slip Covers (Roadster) | $125.00 |
| Slip Covers (5 passenger Touring) | $150.00 |
| Slip Covers (7 passenger Touring) | $175.00 |
| Slip Covers (Limousine) | $200.00 |
| Wood Wheels (Before Erection) | $400.00 |

| Wood Wheels (After Erection) | $550.00 | Victoria Tops (Patent Leather) | $275.00 |
| Victoria Tops (Burbank) | $125.00 | (Extra charge when replacing Touring Tops) | |

*War Tax Extra*

# Studebaker Notes

In the ten-year period from 1925 to 1935, Studebaker introduced a number of innovations. The company claims these American firsts: chromium plating; hard-rubber, steel-cord steering wheels; carburetor silencer; full-power mufflers; helical gears; steel-backed main bearings; and lead bronze connecting rod bearings.

Exactly 160 official endurance and speed records were established by Studebaker cars in 1928.

The company's first cars were electric runabouts and trucks.

The Model C Touring car with top, Studebaker's first gasoline auto, came out in 1904.

Studebaker's emblem was a handsome, white-walled wheel with red showing between the spokes, and the company's name was bannered in diagonal script on top.

The 1916 National Automobile Show boasted a gold chassis, which was valued at $25,000 and exhibited by Studebaker.

In 1954, Studebaker Corp. merged with Packard Motor Car Company to form the Studebaker-Packard Corp.

Pierce-Arrow was sold to Studebaker in 1928.

The last U.S. Studebaker was produced in December 1963.

## Invention of an Era

Olds, Haynes, Ford, the Duryeas, Balzer, Maxim, Winton. . . . Only a handful of men became famous for their pursuits in the early 1890s with what would later be called the automobile. But the fact is that backyard tinkerers all over the country began working on their own horseless-carriage creations at around the same time. Most of them were blissfully unaware that others were doing the same, and most of them were destined to abandon their projects and go unnoticed.

In 1895, the first issue of *Horseless Age* calculated that there were then roughly 300 self-propelled vehicles either planned, built, or in the works in America. (Many were also imported European cars.) Later, old-timers in towns across America stepped forward to claim, at least locally, to have driven the "first automobile." But whether or not the fame rests with the right men, the strange fact remains that the car didn't come forward much sooner. The technology had existed, with steam engines, for more than a century, and trains had been running in the U.S. since 1829.

Hiram Percy Maxim, who planned an automobile in 1892 and had built one by 1895, was one of the few American auto pioneers to later take a stab at explaining the peculiar phenomenon. In 1936, he wrote:

As I look back, I am amazed that so many of us began work so nearly at the same time, and without the slightest notion that others were working on the problem. In 1892, when I began my work on a mechanical road vehicle, I suppose there were 50 persons in the United States working on the same idea.

It has always been my belief that we all began to work on a gasoline-engine-propelled road vehicle at about the same time because it had become apparent that civilization was ready for the mechanical vehicle. It was natural that this idea should strike many of us at about the same time. It has been the habit to give the gasoline engine all the credit for bringing the automobile, as we term the mechanical road vehicle today. In my opinion this is a wrong explanation. We have had the steam engine for over a century. We could have built steam vehicles in 1880, or indeed in 1870. But we did not. We waited until 1895.

The reason why we did not build mechanical road vehicles before this, in my opinion, was because the bicycle had not yet come in numbers and had not directed men's minds to the possibilities of independent, long-distance travel over the ordinary highway. We thought the railroad was good enough. The bicycle could not satisfy the demand which it had created. A mechanically-propelled vehicle was wanted instead of a foot-propelled one, and we now know that the automobile was the answer.*

The use of the term *roots* to describe the beginnings of the American automobile seems apt. No one person could be said to have invented it by himself. Rather, its development is a tangle of related yet disconnected experiments and ideas generated by several representatives of a single growing culture. In other words, the real inventor of the American automobile is America.

# United States Automobile Production Milestones

| YEAR | UNITS PRODUCED |
|------|----------------|
| 1912 | 1 millionth |
| 1920 | 10 millionth |
| 1935 | 50 millionth |
| 1952 | 100 millionth |
| 1960 | 150 millionth |
| 1967 | 200 millionth |
| 1972 | 250 millionth |
| 1979 | 300 millionth |

(Source: MVMA Motor Vehicle Facts & Figures '84)

*Maxim, Hiram Percy. *Horseless Carriage Days* (New York: Harper & Row, 1936).

# Your Favorite Animal

Car names hold a special fascination even for an uninitiated car enthusiast. And animals, inspiring metaphors and similes through the ages, have lent their names to some of the most impressive and controversial automobiles of the last century.

American Bantam
Badger
Barracuda
Beaver
Black Crow
Bobcat
Colt
Cougar
Coyote
Cricket
Crow
Drake
Eagle
Falcon
Fox
Golden Eagle
Great Eagle
Greyhound
Hawk
Honey Bee

Hornet
Impala
Jack Rabbit
Kangaroo
Lark
Lion
Marlin
Mustang
Panther
Petrel
Pinto
Road Runner
Seven Little Buffaloes
Silver Hawk
Stingray
Wasp
Whippet
Wildcat
Wolf
Wolverine

# Look to the Stars

You might think that astronomical car names originated in the space age, but some of these automobiles date from the first decade of automotive history.

| | |
|---|---|
| Comet | Nova |
| Eclipse | Satellite |
| Flying Cloud | Star |
| Galaxie | Starfire |
| Golden Rocket | Sun |
| Jetstar | Sunset |
| Meteor | Vega |
| Moon | |

# Bigger Than Life

Cars, especially early automobiles, represent and always have represented a step up for mankind. Adventures and delights are often associated with these motor machines, so it is no wonder that many of them have been named for creatures and characters from ancient mythology and tall tales.

| | |
|---|---|
| Ajax | Excalibur |
| Apollo | Hercules |
| Argo | Mercury |
| Argonaut | Minerva |
| Atlas | Nike |
| Aurora | Olympian |
| Centaur | Pan |
| Croesus | Sphynx |
| Diana | Vulcan |
| Electra | |

And from literature come these heroically epony-
mous cars:

| | |
|---|---|
| Ariel | Die Valkyrie |
| Ben Hur | Goethe |

# A Sampling of States

Identifying states on a map of the U.S. may be difficult,
but tracking down those automobiles named for our fifty
states is even more of a task. Below is what we consider
to be a complete list.

| | |
|---|---|
| California | New Yorker |
| Carolina | Ohio |
| Illinois | Oregon |
| Indiana | Pennsylvania |
| Maryland | Texan |
| Michigan | Virginian |

State nicknames have also given rise to a few cars:

Bay State                 Keystone
Buckeye                   Lone Star
Empire

# A Sampling of Cities

Proud of your city? Perhaps it is one of the many towns that lent its name to an automobile. Below are only a few examples.

Akron              Milwaukee
Albany             Minneapolis
Birmingham         Niagara
Chicago            Oakland
Cleveland          Omaha
Davenport          Pittsburgh
Detroit            St. Louis
Elgin              Sandusky
Holyoke            Toledo
Indianapolis       Tulsa
Kalamazoo          Waco
Kansas City        Waltham

## AKA: Ford Model T

Here are just a few of the many nicknames popularly conferred on the ubiquitous, unsinkable Ford Model T.

Mechanical Cockroach
Detroit Disaster
Bouncing Betty
Leaping Lena
Galloping Snail
Flivver
Tin Lizzie
Jolting Joni
Spirit of St. Vitus

## A Chronology of the Earliest Steam Cars

| | |
|---|---|
| Father Verbiest's Aeolipile Steam Car | 1655 |
| Sir Isaac Newton's Steam Carriage | 1680 |
| Capt. Nicolas Cugnot's Artillery Tractor | 1763 |
| Dr. Erasmus Darwin's Rotary Motion Steamer | 1765 |
| James Watt's Steam Carriage | 1769 |

| | |
|---|---:|
| William Murdock's "Locomotive" | 1784 |
| Nathan Read's Tubular Boiler | 1790 |
| William Trevithick's Steam Carriage | 1801 |
| Oliver Evans's "Orukter Amphibolos" | 1805 |
| Dumbell's Flash-Type Generator | 1808 |
| Julius Griffith's Steam Carriage | 1821 |
| Burstall and Hill's Steam Carriage | 1824 |
| Nevill's Oscillating Cylinder Carriage | 1825 |
| James and Anderson's Steam Coach | 1829 |
| Summers and Ogle's Multi-Tubular Boiler | 1830 |
| Sir Goldworth Gurney's Steam Coach | 1831 |
| Surrey's Steam Tractor | 1831 |
| William Hancock's "Autopsy" | 1833 |
| Dr. Church's Steam Coach | 1833 |
| John Scott Russell's Steam Car | 1834 |
| Thomas Rickett's Road Steamer | 1858 |
| Richard Dudgeon's Steam Wagon | 1860 |
| Dr. J. N. Carhart's Steam Buggy | 1871 |
| Ransom E. Olds's Steamer | 1887 |
| Stephen Roper's Steam Bicycle | 1894 |
| Frank Vanell's Steam Carriage | 1895 |
| John Einig's Steam Carriage | 1896 |
| A. T. Cross's Steam Carriage | 1897 |
| F. E. and F. O. Stanley's Stanley Steamer | 1897 |

# Production Geography of the American Steam Car

Here is a breakdown of the 18 states and 59 cities in which America's 83 most important steam cars were produced.

| | |
|---|---|
| California | San Francisco |
| Connecticut | Bridgeport, New Haven |
| District of Columbia | Washington |
| Illinois | Elgin, Lanark, Sterling |
| Indiana | Richmond |
| Kansas | Parsons |
| Maine | Brunswick, Lewiston |
| Maryland | Luke |
| Massachusetts | Boston, Chicopee Falls, Danvers, Dorchester, Everett, Marlborough, Newtonville, Orange, Salem, Springfield, Waltham, Westfield, Worcester |
| Michigan | Detroit, Hudson, Jackson |
| Missouri | St. Louis |
| New Hampshire | Keene, Manchester |
| New Jersey | Camden, Passaic, Trenton |
| New York | Amsterdam, Brooklyn, Buffalo, Cohoes, Lockport, Newburgh, New York, Poughkeepsie, Rochester, Syracuse, Tarrytown, Utica |
| Ohio | Cleveland, Columbus, Garfield, Geneva |
| Pennsylvania | Allegheny, Carlisle, New Brighton, Philadelphia, Pittsburgh, Reading |
| Rhode Island | Pawtucket |
| Virginia | Basic |
| Wisconsin | Milwaukee |

# Production Span of Manufactured American Steam Cars

| | | | |
|---|---|---|---|
| American | 1922–1924 | Delling | 1923–1934 |
| American | | Detroit | 1921–1923 |
| Waltham | 1898–1899 | Doble | 1914–1929 |
| Amoskeag | 1867–1906 | Eclipse | 1900–1903 |
| Baker | 1921–1928 | Elite | 1900–1901 |
| Boss | 1903–1907 | Empire | 1904–1905 |
| Binney & | | Foster | 1900–1905 |
| Burnham | 1902–1903 | Gearless | 1921–1923 |
| Brecht | 1902–1904 | Geneva | 1901–1904 |
| Brooks | 1924–1930 | Grout | 1897–1905 |
| Capitol | 1902–1903 | Halsey | 1906–1907 |
| Century | 1899–1902 | Hoffman | 1902–1904 |
| Clark | 1895–1909 | Hood | 1899–1900 |
| Cloughley | 1902–1903 | Howard | 1900–1904 |
| Coats | 1922–1923 | Hudson | 1901–1902 |
| Coldwell | 1903–1905 | Jaxon | 1903–1904 |
| Conrad | 1900–1903 | Jenkins | 1901–1902 |
| Cotta | 1901–1903 | Johnson | 1906–1907 |
| Coulthard | 1905–1906 | Kensington | 1900–1903 |
| Covert | 1901–1904 | Kidder | 1900–1901 |
| Crouch | 1897–1900 | Lane | 1900–1909 |
| Curran | 1928–1929 | Leach | 1899–1900 |
| Dawson | 1901–1902 | Locomobile | 1899–1903 |

| | | | |
|---|---|---|---|
| MacDonald | 1923–1924 | Ross | 1905–1909 |
| Marlboro | 1899–1902 | Scott-Newcomb | 1921–1922 |
| Maryland | 1900–1901 | Skene | 1900–1901 |
| Meteor | 1902–1903 | Stanley | 1897–1925 |
| Milwaukee | 1900–1902 | Steamobile | 1900–1904 |
| Mobile | 1899–1903 | Stearns | 1900–1903 |
| Moncrief | 1901–1902 | Sterling | 1901–1902 |
| Morgan | 1903–1904 | Sunset | 1901–1904 |
| Morse | 1904–1906 | Sweany | 1895–1896 |
| National | 1899–1900 | Toledo | 1901–1903 |
| Neustadt-Perry | 1902–1903 | Tractobile | 1900–1902 |
| New England | 1899–1900 | Twombly | 1904–1905 |
| New York | 1900–1901 | Victor | 1899–1904 |
| Porter | 1900–1901 | Westfield | 1902–1903 |
| Prescott | 1901–1905 | White | 1901–1910 |
| Puritan | 1901–1904 | Whitney | 1898–1905 |
| Reading | 1900–1903 | Whitney | |
| Richmond | 1902–1903 | Automatic | 1897–1898 |
| Rochester | 1900–1901 | Wood | 1902–1903 |
| Roper | 1860–1894 | Wood-Loco | 1901–1902 |

# John "Gunner" Gunnell's Convertible Types

*Landau*
*Convertible* The fixed-position side window frames re-
main erect when the top is lowered. Most
versions have landau irons alongside the
rear quarter section.

**Convertible Cabriolet** The cabriolet is one of the earliest versions of a convertible. In most cases, landau irons were used until about 1932. The side window frames lower with the glass. The top usually folds down to rest upon the rear deck lid.

**Convertible Landau Sedan** Landau styling was used on some four-door models. Only the rear section of the roof is made of cloth and lowers down. This was usually seen on expensive classics but was offered on standard production models, in some lines, for a few years.

**Convertible Coupe (prewar)** As the name implies, the convertible coupe is a soft-top auto made to look like a coupe when the top is raised. The top is designed to be exceptionally weathertight (like the roof on a hardtop coupe).

**Cabriolet Sedan** Similar to a convertible sedan, the cabriolet sedan is a little fancier with landau irons used on the rear quarter of the roof. This can be either a two-door or four-door car.

**Convertible Sedan** The convertible sedan is a four-door convertible with lowerable side windows and a fixed-position windshield frame. A removable support is used at the center of the bodysides to support the top when it is raised.

**Drop-Head Coupe** Usually a foreign version of the convertible coupe, the drop-head coupe is a little fancier with landau irons and, sometimes, a multiposition roof. The drophead is also used on domestic classics with coachbuilt bodies.

**Convertible Coupe (postwar)**  The main difference between prewar and postwar convertible coupes is the seating layout. The postwar coupe is a five-passenger model with a full rear seat.

**Roadster Convertible**  A blend of sporty roadster styling, the roadster convertible has the added advantage of roll-up window glass. Small size and simplicity allow creative roof designs.

**Detachable Hardtop Convertible**  Many open sports cars were available with detachable fiberglass roofs either as standard or optional equipment.

**Retractable Hardtop/ Convertible**  The hardtop/convertible is a very rare style. The most famous example is Ford's Skyliner. The hardtop retracts into the rear of the car.

**Spyder Convertible**  The term *Spyder* is a sports car word and simply describes a small, sporty ragtop— usually with a high-performance engine.

—from *Convertibles: The Complete Story*, by John "Gunner" Gunnell, Blue Ridge Summit, Pennsylvania: TAB Books Inc., 1984

# The Ten Best and Ten Worst

In 1983, *Life* magazine hired a panel of eleven expert car historians, designers, and collectors to decide the 10 best and 10 worst American cars ever. As printed in the September 1983 issue of the magazine, to honor the seventy-fifth anniversary of the General Motors Corporation, here are the results:

## BEST

1. Ford Model T, 1908–1927
2. Curved Dash Olds, 1901–1904
3. Duesenberg SJ, 1932–1933
4. Mercer T Head Raceabout, 1911–1914
5. 1936 Cord 810
6. Pierce-Arrow, 1915–1918
7. Ford Model A, 1903–1931
8. 1955 Chevrolet Bel Air
9. Packard, 1930–1934
10. 1930 Cadillac V–16

## WORST

1. Ford Edsel, 1958–1960
2. Chevrolet Vega, 1970s
3. 1959 Cadillac
4. 1957–58 Packard/Studebaker body
5. 1959 Chevrolet Impala

6. 1957 Mercury Turnpike Cruiser
7. 1958 Buick
8. 1938 Graham Sharknose
9. 1939 Crosley
10. 1957 Nash Ambassador

# America's Forty Best Used Cars of 1985

In June 1985, *Motor Trend* magazine published the results of a survey it did to determine the 40 best used car buys in America. The judging was divided into four categories of auto type (the 10 best in each category), defined as follows: *basic transport*, which held reliability as its number one criterion; *sports/performance*, which were also reliable, but faster and more fun; *bread-and-butter*—good family cars; and *used yacht*—good big cars with style.

As you'll notice, American cars held their own (about 50/50) against foreign makes in the smaller car categories and, perhaps as expected, did much better (8 for 10) in the used-yacht category. Here, in brief, are *Motor Trend's* findings.

## BASIC TRANSPORT

1. Toyota Corolla, 1969–current
2. Plymouth Valiant/Duster, Dodge Dart/Demon, 1964–1976

3. Datsun B210, 210, 1975–current
4. Ford Falcon/Maverick, Mercury Comet, 1966–1977
5. Subaru, 1977–current
6. Volkswagen Beetle, 1960–1978, except 1966
7. Chevrolet Nova, 1968–1977
8. Honda Civic, 1975–current
9. Dodge/Plymouth Colt, 1977–current
10. Ford Fiesta, 1978–1980

Honorable mentions were given in the basic-transport category to the Ford Pinto, 1978–1980, the Mazda GLC, 1977–current, and the Volkswagen Rabbit, 1978–1984.

## SPORTS/PERFORMANCE

1. Chevrolet Corvette, 1953–1982
2. Datsun 240Z/280Z/280ZX, 1970–1983, except 1973–1974 260Z
3. Honda Prelude, 1983–current
4. Ford Mustang, 1964–1973
5. Chevrolet Camaro, 1970½–1981
6. Pontiac Firebird, 1970½–1981
7. Toyota Celica Supra, 1982–current
8. Mazda RX-7, 1979–current
9. BMW 2002, 1968–1975
10. Porsche 911 series, 1965–1979

## BREAD-AND-BUTTER

1. Datsun/Nissan Maxima, 1981–current
2. Volvo 240 DL, 1974–current
3. Olds Cutlass/Buick Regal, 1978–current
4. Toyota Cressida, 1979–current
5. Ford LTD, 1974–1980

6. Chevrolet Malibu/Pontiac LeMans/Oldsmobile Cutlass/Buick Century-Regal, 1973–1977
7. Chevrolet Impala-Caprice/Pontiac Bonneville/ Oldsmobile 88/Buick LeSabre, 1973–current
8. Honda Accord, 1981–current
9. Dodge Aries/Plymouth Reliant, 1981–current
10. Mazda 626, 1979–current

## USED YACHTS

1. Buick Electra/Oldsmobile 98/Cadillac DeVille, 1977–current
2. Cadillac Seville, 1976–1979
3. Lincoln Continental Mark III, 1968–1971
4. Dodge W200 Van, 1970–current
5. Chevrolet Suburban, 1973–current
6. Ford Country Squire Wagon, 1973–current
7. Chrysler Newport/New Yorker, 1979–1981
8. Chevrolet Monte Carlo/Pontiac Grand Prix, 1973–1977
9. Mercedes-Benz 450SEL, 1974–1980
10. Jaguar XJ Sedan/Coupe, 1982–current

# The Ten Worst Used Car Buys of 1985

Here's the logical counterpart of *Motor Trend* magazine's best used car buys list. Also published in *Motor Trend*'s June 1985 issue, the cars in this list were condemned for any number of specific reasons—from having a tendency to overheat to having a smoldering electrical system—but mainly because they're just plain lousy cars.

1. Chevrolet Vega, 1971–1977
2. AMC Pacer, 1975–1980
3. Audi 100 LS, 1970–1977
4. Ford Fairmont/Mercury Zephyr, 1978–1980
5. Porsche 924, 1977–1982
6. Plymouth Volare/Dodge Aspen, 1976–1980
7. General Motors cars equipped with 4.3- and 5.7-liter diesel engines, 1978–1981
8. Triumph TR-7, 1975–1977
9. Fiat 850 Spider, 1968–1972
10. Honda Civic, 1973–1974

# Auto History and Famous Firsts

# Notable Firsts

The first national automobile show was held in 1900 at Madison Square Garden in New York City.

The American Motor League of Chicago was the first auto club, in 1895.

*The Saturday Evening Post* was the first magazine to carry automobile advertisements.

May 25, 1907, marks the day of the first twenty-four-hour race, an endurance derby at Point Breeze, in Philadelphia, Pennsylvania.

A Model T Ford holds the honor as the first auto to be fitted with a car radio, in 1922; this was not the first commercially produced car radio, which appeared in 1927.

The first overdrive transmission is credited to Chrysler in 1934.

The Museum of Modern Art in New York is the first art museum to include a car in its collections. It also has an automobile piston as an example of good design.

Movie buffs point to *The French Connection* and *Bullitt* as the first two modern motion pictures to do justice to a car chase.

## Why "Car"?

The word *car* comes from the Latin *carrus*, a term used to describe the two-wheeled war chariot.

Later it was used to describe any type of chariot, as when Milton (*Comus*) wrote of "the gilded car of day." Soon the term came to include any wheeled vehicle—as when Byron (*Childe Harold's Pilgrimage*) wrote of "the car rattling over the stony street"—and ultimately evolved from describing a horse-drawn carriage to a horseless carriage.

## Why "Automobile"?

It might seem surprising, but when the automobile came suddenly on the American scene in the 1890s, nobody knew what to call it. The word *automobile* hadn't been invented yet. *Horseless carriage* was a disparaging term used by those who didn't like the noisy new contraptions. At the first American auto race in Chicago in 1895, the sponsoring *Times-Herald* called the machines "motocycles," but that was too much like "bicycle" and quickly went by the wayside. Other names suggested were au-tobat, autogen, autogo, autopher, autokinet, ipsometer, autovic, molectro, motor wagon, self-motor, and trun-dler. *Automobile* finally arrived by way of France, where it was invented by members of the French Academy, who had convened especially for that purpose.

# More Notable Firsts

The patent for what we consider an *automobile* was taken out by George Selden on November 5, 1895.

The first automobile accident is said to have occurred on May 30, 1896, in a Duryea car.

*Horseless Age*, which published from 1895 to 1918, was the first automobile magazine.

Alice Huyler Ramsey, Nettie R. Powell, Margaret Atwood, and Hermaine Jahns were the first women to complete a cross-country trip by car. They traveled from New York to San Francisco in a Maxwell-Briscoe from June 9, 1909, to August 6, 1909.

Cadillac introduced the first 16-cylinder engine in the United States in 1930.

Ford Motor Company manufactured the first plastic car in August 1941.

GM Motorama displayed the first gas-turbine engine car, an XP-21 Firebird, in 1954.

William McKinley was the first President to ride in an automobile; his jaunt took place in 1899 in a Stanley steam car.

The World Car by Ford is credited as being the first American subcompact front-wheel-drive car.

## America's First Gas-Powered Automobile

Who made the first gasoline-powered automobile in America?

That, never an easy question to answer, could probably still be argued were a picky historian so inclined.

The final official answer is Charles and Frank Duryea, who together in 1892 built and ran a gas-powered vehicle in Springfield, Massachusetts. But around the turn of the century, at least four other auto manufacturers, including Elwood Haynes, Ransom E. Olds, Alexander Winton, and Henry Ford, stepped forward to claim the honor. They all later backed off, and none of the other more obscure potential claimants ever stepped forward, which left the Duryeas alone as the first.

Originally farmer boys from near Peoria, Illinois, the Duryeas first read about gas-powered horseless carriages in Europe in 1891, while working in Springfield, Massachusetts. The following year, they quit their jobs and went to work on their first car.

Much later, when the brothers had become estranged due to arguments about who was first, Charles claimed that his brother had had nothing to do with the first car built in their shop. However, records show that when Charles left Springfield on a trip to Peoria in mid-1892, Frank assembled the then half-finished car and test-drove it for the first time in November of that year.

That winter, Frank went to work on his second automobile. Built with heavier parts and a more powerful engine, this car made its maiden run through the streets of Springfield on September 22, 1893. While most consider this car the real "first," others believe the 1892 vehicle qualifies as number one. Either way, the brothers have a sound claim to first place.

The Duryeas went on to establish a few other firsts. Soon after building their third auto in 1895, they set up the Duryea Motor Wagon Company of Springfield. And in the winter of 1895/96 they produced 13 Duryeas, which became the first regularly manufactured horseless carriages for sale in the United States.

# America's First Auto Was a Boat, Too

The grand distinction of America's first automobile goes to a vehicle built in 1805 by Oliver Evans of Delaware, Pennsylvania. It was called the Orukter Amphibolis, or Amphibious Digger, and it wasn't really an automobile but a dredge and digging machine commissioned by the Philadelphia Board of Health and designed especially to deepen the docks and waterways of the city.

A massive contraption—30 feet long, 12 feet wide, and weighing in at 35,000 pounds—the Orukter was essentially a flat-bottomed wooden boat with a large steam engine inside and four wheels attached. On land, the vehicle was propelled by a system of belts that turned its wheels, and for treading water, it had a paddle wheel at the rear.

After one abortive attempt to launch the craft, on July 13, Evans successfully steered his machine from its construction site, up Philadelphia's Market Street, around the Central Square, and down to the water's edge, thus making the Orukter Amphibolis the first passenger-carrying, self-propelled vehicle in the United States.

Amid crowds of excited onlookers, Evans and his hissing, clanking machine then lurched into the water, stopped, started again, and eventually chugged one and a half miles up a canal to the city's waterfront. Top speed: four miles per hour.

# Motor-Powered Stagecoach Silences Crack of Whip

Even the high desert towns of the deepest Old West didn't get very old before the automobile moved in. On January 25, 1899, the Everett-King automobile company of Chicago contracted to build nine motor-driven vehicles designed to replace the old stagecoaches that ran between Flagstaff, Arizona, and the Grand Canyon. The sound of the stage driver's "Yeehaw!" and the crack of the whip were doomed.

With a seating capacity of 17 passengers, the new motor coaches were slightly larger than the old ones, but the body designs of the old and new coaches were surprisingly similar: the new coach seated 12 passengers inside and 6 (including the driver) on top. The new coaches were powered by a 14-horsepower gasoline engine, which the builder claimed to be "the most wonderful ever put into a horseless carriage." A few of the new vehicles were smaller in size, with only 8-horsepower engines.

The novel motor stages were contracted in a hurry, with only a sixty-day completion deadline. They were needed for the coming summer, when a National School Teachers' Convention planned to send a thousand teachers to the Grand Canyon.

## Even More Notable Firsts

The first drive-in movie theater opened in 1934 in Camden, New Jersey.

Maryland was the first state to require car inspections, in 1932.

The first Thunderbird premiered in February 1954, at the Detroit Auto Show.

The *Journal of the American Medical Association* issued its first automotive number in April 1910.

The automobile was first used as a hearse in Buffalo, New York, in 1900.

Mechanical windshield wipers first appeared in
the U.S. around 1916; a Willys-Knight car was one of
the pioneers to use them.

The claim of first for a modern hardtop convertible
goes to Buick for its 1949 Riviera.

A 1917 Smith Flyer was the first five-wheeled car.

The XP-500, a General Motors car, is acknowledged as
the first free-piston auto; it was displayed to the
public in May 1956.

# Police, Firemen Get into the Act

America's first police car went to work for the Boston
Police Department in 1903. It was a Stanley Steamer,
with a top speed of about 10 M.P.H. Evidently, it was more
to intimidate criminals than to apprehend them.

The same year, another Stanley Steamer became the
country's first fire engine, in Newton, Massachusetts. It
was an ordinary model car, but it was equipped with
two hand-held fire extinguishers mounted on either side
of the car—approximately enough quenching power to
put out a raging campfire.

# First Car Across America

One day in the spring of 1903, Dr. N. H. Jackson, a physician away from his home of Burlington, Vermont, sat sipping a glass of wine in San Francisco's University Club. Across the room, a group of men were involved in an animated discussion. The growing consensus among the group was that automobiles were fine for short trips around town and such, but for long journeys they were useless. Having overheard this absurd conclusion, Jackson could not help but come to the auto's defense. In his ire, he quickly involved himself in the conversation and punctuated his opposing view with the statement that an automobile could be driven across the continent. Amid guffaws of disbelief, the opposition's leader offered Jackson a wager of fifty dollars if he could prove his claim, and the doctor accepted. Five days later, on May 23, 1903, Jackson and an enthusiastic mechanic from Tacoma, Washington, named Sewall K. Crocker, fired up their 1903 Winton touring car and chugged out of San Francisco on what was to become the first successful crossing of the United States in an automobile.

With difficulty, the Winton climbed over the treacherous roads of the Sierra Nevada, crossed the Great Desert, and headed through the high plains of Idaho, Wyoming, and Nebraska. In many small towns in those states, people had never heard of a car, and as Jackson and Crocker drove down Main Street, cowboys, traders, shepherds, and Indians would stare in amazement. Some people thought it was a little train that had slipped off its rails and gone following horsepaths as if by some instinct.

Poor tires and the scarcity of gasoline were two major impediments to the Winton's headway. Just seven days into the trip, after descending the impossibly rocky roads of the Sierra, the car's rear tires were mostly patches. Unable to get new tires for a time, Jackson finally abandoned the patchwork rubber and ran the wheels on tires made of bundled burlap. Another time, the car ran out of gas on a lonely road in eastern Oregon and Crocker walked 29 miles through the night to get more. But while the roads presented many obstacles, so did some people. One country woman sent the team 54 miles out of their way just so they'd pass her house and let her family see the car.

On July 26, 64 days and roughly 5000 miles after leaving San Francisco, the by-now famous Winton and its exhausted, mud-caked crew pulled up in front of the Holland House at 30th Street and Fifth Avenue, New York City. The Winton had run 45 of 63 days and averaged between 100 and 125 miles a day, despite obstacles and Jackson's claim that "no attempt was made at a speed record." By the end of the trip, however, Jackson had lost 20 pounds and estimated it had cost him $8000 to win the $50 bet.

Back in Burlington a short time later, Jackson became the first man ever arrested in that town for driving a car over the 6-mile-per-hour speed limit. He was fined $5.

# This Car Climbed Mt. Washington

Conquering mountains with the automobile started as early as August 31, 1899, when Mr. and Mrs. F. O. Stanley drove their Stanley Steamer to the summit of New Hampshire's 6288-foot Mt. Washington, making theirs the first horseless buggy ever to complete the grueling climb. The trip took 2 hours and 10 minutes, including stops. It was more than three years before the first gasoline-powered car made the same climb, in September 1902. However, the Stanley Steamers triumphed again, when F. E. Stanley, the pioneer conqueror's twin, took a Model EX up the mountain in a mere 27 minutes.

# Central Park Admits First Automobile

In its infancy, the automobile in America was considered by many to be a noisy and bothersome contraption. Early car owners felt that those who didn't own cars held a distinct prejudice for those who did. George C.

Clausen, commissioner of New York's Central Park in 1899, was accused of such prejudice for his decree restricting autos from the park. But soon the persuasive efforts of motoring enthusiasts convinced Clausen and other disbelievers of the automobile's compatibility with even the most fashionable environments.

On Sunday, November 13, 1899, Clausen accepted the invitation of one R.A.C. Smith to ride in Smith's electric automobile through the park. A cordon of policemen on horseback surrounded the automobile in anticipation of runaway carriages, and the Sunday crowds were reportedly astonished at the curious procession. No mishaps occurred, however, until Mr. Smith, in his eagerness to demonstrate all the things his car could do, ended the excursion by causing a vital part of the car to break. Smith and Clausen had to walk home. Nonetheless, Clausen was impressed and issued to Mr. Smith the first permit to drive a car in the park.

# Liberated Woman Drives Car in Central Park

The women's liberation movement of the twentieth century will never point to the name of Florence E. Woods as one of its greatest contributors. However, this energetic young woman did achieve an interesting first for women, as well as for automotive history.

On January 2, 1900, the seventeen-year-old Miss Woods became the first woman allowed to drive a car in New York's Central Park. In the previous weeks, she had frequently been seen cruising the streets of the Upper East Side in her little electric knockabout built for two, but she was determined to expand her territories to the park. Park officials denied her first request for a permit to drive in the park, but she persisted. A few days later, she gave the park secretary a personal demonstration of her expertise behind the wheel. He was duly impressed, and Miss Woods got her permit.

"I am astonished that women seem so timid," Miss Woods told *The New York Times*. "Any girl could operate [an automobile] as easily as she could drive a pony."

Miss Woods is said to have caused quite a sensation when she first appeared in her car along Fifth Avenue. Coachmen looked on with amazement, and some made unpleasant remarks. But Miss Woods ignored them all and went happily on her way.

## Bet You Didn't Know

Charles Duryea hired his brother Frank to work on the first American auto—for $3 a day.

Legend has it that the first carburetor was Charles Duryea's wife's perfume atomizer.

E. B. White and Richard Lee Strout wrote a short story about the Model T Ford under the pseudonym Lee Strout White. The story, "Farewell, My Lovely," appeared in the *New Yorker* magazine in 1936.

The man most often associated with the phrase "Gentlemen, start your engines" is Anton "Tony" Hulman, Jr. (1901–1977).

What do the Aircar, Airphibian, Arrowbile, Convair-car, Jetmobile, and Roadable have in common?
They were all built to be flying cars.

Helen Ford, a well-known actress of her day, was "the first of her sex to receive a new Ford," according to one Boston newspaper.

The National Bowling Hall of Fame and Museum in St. Louis has a car in its collection: a Pin Car, a giant bowling pin on wheels that had once been a standard 1936 Studebaker coupe.

The Indianapolis Motor Speedway Hall of Fame has one of the most extensive collections of old car photographs in the world.

Ronald Reagan, as a representative of the General Electric Company, attended the 1954 Chicago Auto Show as a special celebrity guest.

The Thunderbird was advertised as a "Mink Coat for Father."

## Interesting Facts

More than 2200 different makes of automobile have been manufactured in the U.S.

Of the 909 automobiles registered in New York State in 1902, 485 were steam powered, 424 gas powered.

More than 100 different makes of electric car were manufactured in the U.S.

More than 125 different makes of steam car were manufactured in the U.S.

At least 82 different makes of car have been manufactured in Cleveland, Ohio.

The 1905 Twyford, built in Brookville, Pennsylvania, was the first 4-wheel drive car in the U.S.

In 1921, Texas had 15,932 miles of highway roads, more than any other state.

In 1895, 4 cars were produced in U.S. In 1929, more than 4 million were made in America.

In 1900, the cities of New York, Boston and Chicago had 2,370 automobiles combined: 1,170 steam, 800 electric, 400 gas.

# Lost and Found

After a brief but famous career, America's first gas-powered buggy, built in 1893 by Frank and Charles Duryea, disappeared. Around 1900, in the wake of the new car boom, the dated buggy somehow drifted into total obscurity and was from that point on never heard of or seen. Roughly twenty-three years passed before the old prototype was discovered in a barn in Springfield, under a heavy shroud of dust and cobwebs. Its metal parts were covered with rust, its leather upholstery dry and cracked. The car was eventually completely restored, and it now sits in the Smithsonian Institution in Washington, D.C.

# Average Total Cost of Operating an Automobile 1950–1983

| YEAR | COST PER MILE |
|------|---------------|
| 1983 | 33.42¢ |
| 1982 | 32.35¢ |
| 1981 | 31.92¢ |
| 1980 | 27.95¢ |
| 1975 | 16.62¢ |
| 1969 | 14.48¢ |
| 1965 | 11.77¢ |
| 1960 | 11.99¢ |
| 1955 | 9.53¢ |
| 1950 | 8.61¢ |

(Source: *MVMA Motor Vehicle Facts & Figures '84*)

# A Glance Through Topics

Distinctly interesting are these AUTOMOBILE TOPICS,
That reach across the continents, and from the poles to
    tropics;
"Society," and "Clubs," and "Sports," with "Topics," make a
    showing
Of all within this auto-world, that's rolling, whizzing, going,
Of what to get, and how to get, and when to get, the
    needful,
For outing, racing, journeying, and all that's swell and
    speedful.
You learn who's "it," and what they do, at home or 'cross
    the oceans;
Of all that's newest, best and fit; the knowledge and the
    notions
Of everything you need to know concerning auto-wheeling,
And all this glorious sport, that's good to end that "tired
    feeling."
Therein you learn "Haynes-Apperson" present a runabout
That's nearly worth its weight in gold—a gem, without
    a doubt;
That "Winton" cars have set the pace across betwixt the
    seas,
And "Oldsmobile's" a hummer, while all the world agrees
That "Peerless," for good service, is rightly christened so,
And "Darracq" is a wonder for a tourist—"don-cher-know?"
The "Locomobile's" shown to be, by choosers, sudden
    choice,

And "Banker Brothers" sell the cars that make the heart
  rejoice;
The "Cadillac" shines brightly, a star of dazzling ray,
And the "Buffalo's" a treasure, forever and a day.
Then here is Pope's "Toledo," the "Waverly" and "Yale,"
Machines that stand the racket and are never known to fail.
The "Rambler" and the "Franklin," the "Pierce" and the
  "White,"
With strength and speed, endurance and elegance unite.
The "Columbia" and "Richard," the "Searchmont" and
  "Elmore,"
Have records and endorsements and qualities galore.
The "Studebaker" stands high up, "De Dietrich" has renown,
"Pope-Robinson" and "Premier" and "Baker's" wear a
  crown.
Soon Messrs. Smith & Mabley will open wide your eyes,
With the "C.G.V."—a beauty and a glorious surprise.
A wonder is the new "Clement," says Mason, who should
  know;
He only sells to swelldom here, his cars are "all the go."
The "Chicago Motor Company" has "Money-Maker" fame,
And the "Central's" importations have a high and well-
  earned name.
The "Autocar of Ardmore" leaves nothing to desire,
But here's a "Goodrich Clincher," discussing rubber tire,
With one who dotes on "Diamonds," in a way that is terrific,
For he's bragging of his journey to Atlantic from Pacific,
With "Goodyear" and the "Stodders," "G & J." and others,
With "bithulitic" waterproof, make any wheeling jolly,
And here is "Charlie Miller," sure cure for melancholy.
He'll sell you anything on earth, as sure as you are born,
From a motor to a sparking plug, a hammer or a horn;
For with the trade he stands "A1," straight up and down and
  "hunki,"
And another one along that line is brother A. H. Funke.

---

Here's "Demmerle" to dress you up, "Salamandrine" for
    boilers,
"Charlie Splitdorf" coils around, the "Dixon" folks are oilers;
The "Veeders" tell how far you go, the "Standard" sells
    you rims,
The "Solar" lamps of "Badger" fame will fit you for the glims;
"DeDion Bouton Company" and "Witherbee's Ignition,"
With batteries and motors, are in the best condition.
But grab your "'Gyptian Deity"—Here's Mr. Kenneth
    Skinner,
The Boston "Storage" man—let's go with Robertson to
    dinner—
He "Auto Change" a feed for this, and faith, I think he will,
For here's what any man would call—a four flush? No, a fill.

—from *The Automobile* magazine, 1903

## Coming or Going?

Among the most remarkable trips in American automobile history must be included that of Charles Creighton and James Hargis. In 1930, they drove a Model A Ford Roadster from New York to Los Angeles and back again—all without stopping the engine once. It took them 42 days to complete the 7180-mile round trip, which may not sound all that fast, but consider this: The entire journey was driven in reverse.

# More Interesting Facts

The Edsel lost approximately $250 million, over a three-season period, for Ford.

It was a Packard touring car that was disguised as a police vehicle in the St. Valentine's Day Massacre in 1929.

In 1985, Dana Corporation's precision control division announced that it developed a voice-activated cruise control.

The exterior paint job on an average American car uses two gallons; the prime, one gallon.

The word *convertible* did not become a standardized term (by the Society of Automotive Engineers) within the auto industry until 1928.

The Cord emblem supposedly originated from Scotland's M'Cord or Mackorda clan.

The Stanley survived longer than any other American-made steam car.

The year 1978 marked the beginning of a tradition; that was the first year of the Meadow Brook Concours

d'Elégance, a competition to choose the most elegant
car represented.

The 1904 Stanley Steamer got 16 miles per gallon if
gasoline was used, and 20 miles per gallon
on paraffin.

## Body Styles

**Brougham**   This luxury automobile designation refers
to a town car with a closed metal rear
compartment (see *Town Car*). Rear quarter
windows are sometimes associated with
these styles.

**Cabriolet**   Also called a convertible coupe (see
*Coupe*). Rumble seats, luggage racks, and
side mounts are often found in these convertible models.

**Coupe**   These are enclosed cars, usually with two
doors, side windows, and a trunk. Busi-
ness coupes are shorter than club coupes,
which can usually seat up to five passengers.

**Limousine**   A large luxury sedanlike automobile, it
sometimes is built with a glass partition
between the driver's seat and the passenger compartment; the car is often chauf-
feur-driven.

**Phaeton**      These five-passenger cars sometimes offer additional space for passengers on fold-down seats. The term designates a roomy, open car.

**Roadster**    Also called a runabout. All roadsters are open cars, some with a folding or removable top and side curtains. A rumble seat present changes the car's designation to a sport roadster. Most roadsters—with or without a rumble seat—are sporty and relatively small.

**Sedan**       This term applies to all cars with a fixed top that hold at least four passengers in one compartment with full bench seats. The postwar two-door sedan is also known as a pillared coupe.

**Station Wagon**    A larger-than-sedan-size car, this style often features back seats that can be moved, folded, or otherwise manipulated to form an interior space useful for light trucking. Usually, no additional storage space is offered, and there is often a tailgate.

**Touring Car**    Also called a Tourabout. This car, popular in the twenties, is an open-type automobile that seats four, five, or seven.

**Town Car**    This auto designation is a variation on the limousine; the car has an open, removable, or folding top. Town cars with fixed fabric roofs on the rear quarter have also been called cabriolets.

---

# R. E. Olds Tells All

Ransom E. Olds had a vision when it came to his cars; he knew what he wanted, and he wanted his customers to care for their new cars properly. Here are a few of his "rules" from the instruction book that accompanied the cars:

1. Don't make "improvements" without first writing the factory.
2. Don't drive your Oldsmobile more than 100 miles on the first day. You wouldn't drive a green horse 10 miles till you were acquainted with him. Do you know more about a gasoline motor than you do about a horse?
3. Don't take anybody's word for it that your tanks have plenty of gasoline and water and your cup plenty of oil. They may be guessing.
4. Don't confess that you are less intelligent than those driving Oldsmobiles. We make the only motor that "motes."

# The Next Time You Hit a Bump, Say Thank You!

The automobile tire as we know it seems an uncomplicated thing: a simple piece of rubber fitted to a metal rim and filled with air. But actually, the development of pneumatic rubber tires was almost as slow and complex as that of the automobile itself. Throughout their histories, the advances of the automobile and rubber tire industries have been inseparably linked. In fact, it could be argued that without the discovery and refinement of the rubber tire, the automobile would have remained little more than an amusing novelty.

Why? Because the unyielding metal wheels used on early autos were so uncomfortable that very few people could stand to ride on them for long. Combined with bad roads and rigid suspensions, metal wheels could rattle a body senseless in short order.

It was the rubber tire—first solid, then air-filled—that transformed the new motor buggy into a viable form of transportation. Here are some of the milestones in its evolution:

• The acknowledged father of the rubber industry was an American named Charles Goodyear, who in 1830 undertook experiments to transform raw rubber into a more solid, usable product. He started by buying, on credit, a load of raw rubber from a shoe factory. When he couldn't pay the debt, he was thrown in debtor's prison, and it was there that he actually began his experiments. After serving his sentence, Goodyear continued his experiments without success until 1839. One winter night that year, Goodyear gathered some friends at his house in order to raise funds so that he might continue his work. He showed them a ball of gum rubber, the surface of which he had managed to harden by mixing it with sulfur and treating it with an acid-gas, thus proving his progress. In the enthusiasm of his demonstration, Goodyear accidentally flung the ball of rubber into a hot wood stove. As he scraped it off with a knife, he discovered it had hardened to the perfect consistency. Then and there was born the process known as vulcanization—and the rubber tire industry along with it.

• An English blacksmith by the name of Robert William Thomson got the first patent for a pneumatic rubber tire in 1845. His tire was essentially a hollow tube made from strips of rubber-coated canvas. He covered them with leather for durability, but that wasn't enough. Word quickly got around among coach drivers that Thomson's newfangled product didn't last more than a few miles and was susceptible to blowouts that scared horses out of their wits. Thomson's patent went to the back files—permanently.

• John Boyd Dunlop, a veterinarian in Belfast, Ireland, reinvented the pneumatic rubber tire in 1888, unaware of Thomson's earlier invention. Dunlop undertook the project—crafting tires from linen-covered sheet rubber— in an attempt to make his son's bicycle more ridable. He was granted a patent for "an improvement in tyres . . . for bicycles and tricycles." One year later, in 1889, Dunlop sold his idea to Harvey du Cros, Jr., who established the Dunlop Rubber Company. Dunlop himself was never part of the company.

• The first rubber tire maker to approach the infant automobile industry with the idea of air-filled tires was a Frenchman named André Michelin. In 1895, Michelin entered a car outfitted with pneumatics in a 350-mile race from Paris to Bordeaux. Unfortunately, the car had at least 22 flats along the way, and the air-filled tire was pronounced a failure. M. Levassor, part-owner and driver of the car that won the race on solid rubber tires, said afterward: "Tyres filled with hay or straw might be successful, but never if filled with air." Levassor's forecast held true for 16 years. In the meantime, tire manufacturers tried not only hay and straw for tire filling, but also cork, glue, syrup, glycerine, arsenic, sand, sawdust, rawhide, rags, and even tennis balls!

• The greatest breakthrough for a viable pneumatic tire was made in 1894 by a New York businessman and scientist called Alexander Straus. He devised a process by which fabrics could be made to stretch in one direction but not the other. Seventeen years later, in 1911, Straus's son, Philip, discovered his father's patent for the process in the family archives. At the time, Philip was treasurer for the Hardman Tire & Rubber Company, and he immediately realized the importance of the invention. Soon, the Hardman Company was producing the first combination tire and tube; that is, an air-filled inner tube and a hard rubber outer casing reinforced with the Straus fabric.

• In 1903, P. W. Litchfield of the Goodyear Tire Company received a patent for the first tubeless tire—one that integrated the 2-piece arrangement introduced by the Hardman company 8 years later—but it was an idea that remained on the shelf for 51 years, until 1954, when a Packard came out with tubeless tires.

• In 1908, Frank Seiberling perfected a machine that cut grooves in the tire surface for better traction. Up to that point, car tires had been smooth as a modern bicycle tire inner tube, making traction impossible if the roads were bad, which they almost always were. It was normal for motorists to carry rags, ropes, and cables to wrap around their tires if they got stuck in a mud puddle or such.

• In 1904, the first demountable wheel rim was introduced on a car called the Christie. The removable rim allowed motorists to repair flat tires on the roadside.

Since its beginnings, the tire industry's primary aim has been the improvement of materials to make stronger tires. For example, in 1910 B. F. Goodrich introduced a tire that incorporated a rugged new fiber material rather than ordinary fabric. Two years later, the same company added large amounts of carbon to the rubber to increase abrasion resistance. By 1920, the life expectancy of auto tires had tripled, to about 13,000 miles.

As World War II neared, shipping lanes to the natural rubber plantations of Southeast Asia and South America were cut off by the threat of submarines. Thus, both America and Germany began research on petroleum-based synthetic rubber. Goodyear started making semi-synthetic tires in 1937, having patented a man-made rubber called Chemigum as far back as 1927.

By the mid-1950s man-made rubber accounted for one half of all U.S. tire production. Today, the average automobile tire is 60 percent synthetic, 40 percent natural.

# Milestones in the Age of the Auto

When the first National Auto Show opened in New York City on November 3, 1900, the automobile was scarcely more than a rumor to most Americans, but enlightenment quickly followed. Curious crowds poured into Madison Square Garden by the thousands, and journalists from all over were there to report on what was then most widely known as the sport of automobiling.

The spectators, according to one reporter for *The New York Times*, were a varied lot. "There were experts," the reporter wrote, "those who can tell at a glance a gasoline vehicle from one propelled by steam or electricity. Then there were the devotees of the new sport, critical examiners of the confusingly many styles and makes of motor wagons. There were society people and other fashionables, many of them intent upon purchase, and seeking wisdom by careful comparison of the different manufacturers' wares."

For the exposition, a 200-foot long, 53-foot high ramp was erected on the roof of the Garden for hill-climbing demonstrations and braking tests. Inside, a wooden track, 20 feet wide and ⅛ of a mile long, circled the main exhibit area, where 40 manufacturers displayed some 300 models. Lack of space necessitated the building of a large platform on top of the spectator boxes.

"Here are located the booths of the manufacturers of

the numberless accessories to the machines," the article said, going on to add that there were, "rubber tires of all kinds, special brakes, improved appliances for the various motors of standard make, and other queer contrivances which make the layman to pause in puzzled wonder and the young men in charge of the odd exhibits to grow eloquent in explanation."

Cars at the show ranged in price from $280 to $4,000, most being closer to the latter figure and, thus, far out of reach for the average person. Accordingly, "the smart set were present in noticeable numbers," the *Times* reporter wrote.

*Motor World*, an early auto publication, spent more words on the elitist bent of the show, criticizing the apparent snobbiness of the early automotive "in" crowd, calling them, "self-constituted arbiters of all automobilism and an aristocracy or autocracy to whose sacred membership no man without cerulean sanginaceousness or millionairish pretensions is to be eligible."

In a few short years, however, cars were popping up all over the place. The auto show turned into an event more for the common man, and innovation was the key. Here are some of the more noteworthy milestones of the show:

**1903:** The closed car made its debut, as did the glass windshield.

**1904:** Steering wheels made tillers all but obsolete.

**1908:** A Packard two-seater featured the first rumble seat. It was called "the honeymoon car."

**1909:** The compressed-air self-starter was introduced, and probably made a splash at the time, but it never worked very well. It would be another three years before the electric self-starter as we know it today was perfected by its inventor, Samuel Kettering.

**1914:** Henry Ford announced during the show a $5 daily

minimum wage for his workers. His employees should be able to afford the cars they built, he said.

**1916:** The needs of the female customer were given new attention. Car interiors now featured vanity cases, clocks, crystal flower vases, telephones to direct the driver, and smelling salts.

**1917:** Heaters made their first appearance on many models.

**1920:** Flat tires became possible for the first time: the pneumatic tire was introduced.

**1922:** Like no other car till then, the Wills-St. Claire had a back-up light.

**1925:** An old car to the show, called the Ambassador, appeared with a new idea attached. Now it was called the Hertz "Drivurself," the first car for rental purposes.

**1926:** Stutz and Rickenbacker models featured "shock-proof" glass.

**1927:** The inaugural year for chrome trim.

**1930:** The Gardner, the Cord, and the Auburn all offered front-wheel drive. It wasn't exactly new, since there had been front-wheel-drive cars before the turn of the century, but these were the first front-wheel drives widely available to the public.

**1931:** Interior sun visors made their debut. During the show, the National Automobile Chamber of Commerce passed a decree that new model announcements be limited to November and December for "the greatest benefit to the public and the dealers."

**1933:** Fuel economy was a concern with manufacturers for the first time, and several displays incorporated billboards with mileage claims.

**1937:** The automatic transmission as it is known today appeared on an Oldsmobile, and many manufac-

---

turers moved their batteries to a strange new position—under the hood.

**1938:** Buick came out with the turn signal.

The show was suspended with the outbreak of World War II. After 1939, it didn't happen again until 1956, when it resumed a few blocks uptown, at the new New York Coliseum.

## Automotive Hall of Fame Electees

| ELECTEE/YEARS ELECTED | DISTINCTIONS |
| --- | --- |
| Don Allen/1974 | Production, sales, and service innovator; creator of the "Dealer Operation" plan |
| John W. Anderson/1972 | Founder of the Anderson Company, which designed and patented many products for Anco |
| Vincent Bendix/1984 | Designed and built Bendix Motor Buggies; manufactured Bendix starter drives; was the first to offer the U.S. auto industry a reliable four-wheel brake system |

| | |
|---|---|
| Carl Benz/1984 | Patented the world's first gasoline-powered vehicle; established the first automotive production line |
| Robert Bosch/1984 | Founded the Bosch Magneto Company and developed one of the earliest automobile lighting systems, the auto horn, the magneto, and the diesel injection pump |
| Ernest R. Breech/1979 | Credited with the transformation of Ford from a company that was losing money to an expanding, aggressive leader in the automobile industry |
| Carl Breer/1976 | Conceived the ideas behind Chrysler's Air-Flow automobiles, among many other automotive credits |
| David D. Buick/1974 | Founded the Buick Motor Car Company and perfected the valve-in-head engine |
| Walter R. Carey/1981 | Organized Commercial Carriers, Inc. and served as a member on the board or as an advisor to many public |

| | and government organizations |
|---|---|
| Albert C. Champion/1977 | Organized the Champion Ignition Company with W. C. Durant (which later became a part of General Motors) |
| Roy D. Chapin/1972 | Formed the Hudson Motor Car Company and served as Secretary of Commerce under President Hoover |
| Roy D. Chapin, Jr./1984 | Credited with introducing many successful lines of cars at American Motors, where he served as chairman |
| Louis Chevrolet/1969 | Raced in many early automobile contests; lent his name to Chevrolet Motor Company and founded Frontenac Motor Corp. |
| Walter P. Chrysler/1967 | Reorganized the Maxwell-Chalmers company, which eventually became Chrysler Corp.; organized the DeSoto Motor Corp.; and acquired the Dodge Brothers Company |
| Edward N. Cole/1977 | Helped to develop Cadillac's short stroke V-8 |

| ELECTEE/YEARS ELECTED | DISTINCTIONS |
| --- | --- |
|  | engine and other automotive design and engineering advancements; served as president of General Motors |
| E. L. Cord/1976 | Acquired controlling interest in the Auburn Automobile Company; purchased control of Duesenberg, Inc. |
| Frederick C. Crawford/1983 | Founded Thompson Products, a small auto parts manufacturer, which became TRW; established the Frederick C. Crawford Auto-Aviation Museum |
| Clessie L. Cummins/1973 | Introduced the automotive diesel to the United States; founded the Cummins Engine Company |
| Harlow H. Curtice/1971 | Expanded and modernized Buick's plants; joined General Motors as executive vice-president |
| Gottlieb Daimler/1978 | Granted a patent for a motor carriage in 1886; founded the Daimler Motors Corp. |
| Charles A. Dana/1978 | Served on the staff of two New York District |

| | |
|---|---|
| | Attorneys; was elected to the state legislature; saved the Universal Joint Manufacturing Company from bankruptcy (now the Dana Corp.) |
| Ralph DePalma/1973 | Won over 2,557 of his 2,889 races, including the Vanderbilt Cup, Elgin, Illinois, Grand Prix, and Indianapolis |
| Rudolf Diesel/1978 | Built and developed the diesel engine and founded the Diesel Motor Company of America |
| Arthur O. Dietz/1983 | Dubbed "the Father of the Installment Credit" plan; was a founding member of the Automotive Safety Foundation |
| Abner Doble/1972 | Operated the Abner Doble Motor Vehicle Company of Waltham, Massachusetts, and later established Doble Steam Motors Corp. |
| Horace E. Dodge/1981 | Produced the first Dodge at Dodge Brothers, Inc.; inventor of special machinery to be used in the building of recoils |
| Fred S. Duesenberg/1970 | Raced at Indianapolis in |

| ELECTEE/YEARS ELECTED | DISTINCTIONS |
| --- | --- |
| | 1913 and 1914; established the Duesenberg Motor Company and the Duesenberg Automobile and Motors Company; designed the first American-built straight-8 engine |
| William C. Durant/1968 | Reorganized the Durant-Dort Carriage Company to become the Buick Motor Car Company; launched General Motors Company; founded Durant Motors; known also as Chevrolet's "Fabulous Billy" |
| Charles E. Duryea/1973 | Collaborated with his brother to build the first Duryea car |
| Joseph O. Eaton/1983 | Developed a reliable truck axle and founded the Eaton Corporation |
| Thomas A. Edison/1969 | Perfected the first nickel-iron-alkaline battery for use in automobiles; held 1079 patents, of which 356 dealt with electric generation, distribution, and lighting |
| Harvey S. Firestone, Sr./1974 | Formed the Firestone Tire & Rubber Company; pioneered in making |

| ELECTEE/YEARS ELECTED | DISTINCTIONS |
| --- | --- |
| Harvey S. Firestone, Jr./1975 | pneumatic tires for the Model T Ford Expanded the Firestone Tire & Rubber Company's interests overseas; was national chairman of United Service Organizations, Inc. and was awarded the highest honor that the Department of Defense can give to civilians who are not directly in government service |
| Carl G. Fisher/1971 | Built the Indianapolis Speedway as well as tracks in Miami Beach and Montauk Point |
| Edsel Ford/1968 | Sparked the Ford styling revolution of the 1950s; supervised Ford's participation in public events; served as president of the company |
| Henry Ford/1967 | Helped organize the Detroit Automobile Company; organized and became president of the Ford Motor Company; known as the father of the assembly line |
| Henry Ford II/1983 | Served as CEO and chairman of Ford; |

| | |
|---|---|
| | increased the company's net income from \$11 million in 1945 to a high of \$1.7 billion in 1977 |
| Herbert H. Franklin/1972 | Started the Franklin Automobile Company |
| Carlyle Fraser/1981 | Transformed the Genuine Parts Company into a profitable business; became a key figure in the National Automotive Parts Association |
| Thomas N. Frost/1970 | Entered state politics and was active on the Governor's Budget Commission (Virginia) on rules, roads, and interstate cooperation |
| Martin E. Goldman/1981 | Known as the dean of the Automotive Aftermarket industry; developed and conducted many advertising programs |
| Richard H. Grant/1971 | Credited as increasing Chevrolet's sales fivefold |
| Zenon C. R. Hansen/1983 | Elected chairman of Mack Trucks and accomplished major changes there through quality control |
| William E. Holler/1969 | Established a number of outstanding sales programs that set sales records at Chevrolet |

| ELECTEE/YEARS ELECTED | DISTINCTIONS |
| --- | --- |
| Anton Hulman, Jr./1978 | Developed the Indianapolis Motor Speedway into the world's premier auto racing facility |
| Thomas B. Jeffery/1975 | Credited with the first clincher tire and an early automobile carburetor; founded the Thomas B. Jeffery Company, which, after a series of changes, became the American Motors Corporation |
| K. T. Keller/1971 | Served as president and chairman of the Chrysler Corporation |
| Charles F. Kettering/1967 | Developed and helped perfect the ignition system and electric starter; was considered the man behind quick-drying lacquer, harmonic balancers, four-wheel brakes, headlamps, two-way shock absorbers, and many more inventions necessary to the auto industry |
| William S. Knudsen/1968 | Known as a production genius within the auto world; elected president of General Motors; was awarded the |

| ELECTEE/YEARS ELECTED | DISTINCTIONS |
| --- | --- |
| | army's Distinguished Service Medal |
| Edward C. Larson/1984 | Served as president of the Anderson Company (ANCO) |
| Henry M. Leland/1973 | Started Leland, Faulconer, and Norton, which became Leland and Faulconer; founded the Cadillac Automobile Company and Lincoln Motor Company |
| Paul Weeks Litch- field/1984 | Became president of Goodyear Tire & Rubber Company and started the Goodyear Research Laboratory |
| John M. "Jack" Mack/1972 | Commercialized the first 4-cylinder sightseeing bus; formed Mack Trucks, Inc. in its infancy; dubbed "the Father of our Great Interstate System" |
| Brouwer D. McIntyre/1975 | Led the Monroe Auto Equipment Company to greater success; served on the War Production Board for the U.S. govern- ment during World War II |
| Robert Samuel McLaughlin/1973 | Was a partner in the McLaughlin Motor Car Company, which produced the McLaughlin- |

| ELECTEE/YEARS ELECTED | DISTINCTIONS |
| --- | --- |
| | Buick and later became part of General Motors; served as president and chairman of the board of General Motors of Canada |
| Charles Stewart Mott/1973 | Credited with streamlining General Motors production; mayor of Flint, Michigan |
| Charles W. Nash/1975 | Became president of Buick and the leader of the Oakland Motor Company, Olds Motor Works, General Motors Truck Company, and General Motors; founded the Nash Motor Company |
| B. E. "Barney" Oldfield/1968 | One of the first known documented auto racers, winning first place in the Daytona and Indianapolis races among many others |
| Ransom E. Olds/1968 | Holder of more than 224 pages of patents; founder of Oldsmobile and Reo auto companies |
| Edward V. Rickenbacker/1973 | World-renowned as a race car driver; started the Rickenbacker Motor Car Company; owned the Indianapolis |

| ELECTEE/YEARS ELECTED | DISTINCTIONS |
| --- | --- |
| Willard F. Rockwell, Sr./1980 | Motor Speedway at one time Led and diversified Timken-Detroit Axle Company, Standard Steel Spring Company, and Rockwell Manufacturing Company; helped to create Rockwell International Corporation |
| Louis Schwitzer, Sr./1970 | Won the first Indianapolis 500; is credited as the designer of the turbocharger, thermostatic controls, and pressure oil pumps |
| Alfred P. Sloan, Jr./1967 | Helped found United Motors, which General Motors took over; became president of General Motors |
| John W. Stokes/1970 | Edited Stokes Tax Controls, Inc., a newsletter for automobile dealers; became known as a speaker on profit-and-loss plans for the automotive industry |
| Robert A. Stranahan, Sr./1979 | Founded the Champion Spark Plug Company with his brother |
| Walter C. Teagle/1974 | Was president and chairman of the board of the Standard Oil |

| | Company; advanced the oil industry overseas |
| --- | --- |
| Henry H. Timken, Sr./1977 | Helped to establish the Timken Company and develop and patent the tapered roller bearing |
| Edwin J. Umphrey/1974 | Credited with building a strong dealer organization for General Motors in Canada |
| Col. Jesse G. Vincent/1971 | Awarded 206 patents; helped to establish Packard's Twin 6, Straight 8, and V-12 engines; the Rolls-Royce engine of the early '40s; and the "299" and "905" engines for race cars |
| J. Irving Whalley/1981 | Elected to the Pennsylvania and U.S. legislature, where he promoted automotive programs |
| John L. Wiggins/1975 | Known for his work with ASIA and especially the Automotive Advertisers Council |
| C. Harold Wills/1970 | Designed the Ford Model A and is credited with coming up with the Ford script; built the Wills-St. Claire; established himself as a leader in the field of automotive metallurgy |

# Headlights

# Elwood Haynes

Elwood Haynes is an odd bird among automobile pioneers. Whereas most early car makers were mere backyard tinkerers or self-styled engineers, Haynes actually held a graduate engineering degree in metallurgy, having studied at Worcester Polytech and Johns Hopkins. After a short time as a schoolteacher, Haynes moved to Kokomo, Indiana, where he worked as a field superintendent for a natural gas company. The frustration of long hours spent plodding around the county in a horse-drawn buggy sparked Haynes into drawing up plans for a gas-powered buggy like he'd read were being made in France.

In the fall of 1893, having finished his plans, Haynes bought a single-cylinder gas engine and a buggy body and hired the services of Elmer Apperson, a local machine-shop owner. Apperson was dubious about the project at first, but he soon took a keen interest and made suggestions of his own, as did his brother Edgar, a bicycle repairman. Within months, the auto was ready to roll. On July 4, 1894, with a sizable crowd of onlookers, Haynes and Apperson drove the horseless buggy one and a half miles out of town and back at the blistering pace of 7 M.P.H. "We flew down the Pumpkinville Pike," said Haynes in describing the maiden run. Haynes and Apperson went on to become partners in one of the first auto manufacturing plants in America.

# Ransom E. Olds

Ransom Eli Olds first got interested in self-powered vehicles while working as a mechanic in his father's machine shop in Lansing, Michigan. Although his father's shop specialized in making gasoline engines, Olds's first auto creation was a steam-powered tricycle, which he drove through the streets of Lansing in 1887. In 1893, a year after taking over his father's business, Olds completed a second auto, also steam-powered but a four-wheeler. The car was favorably reviewed in *Scientific American* and thus came to the attention of a company in Bombay, India, which made Olds an offer on the auto. It was accepted, and Olds made his (and his country's) first auto sale.

Olds built his first gas-powered car in 1896 and by then had determined to go into the auto business. Three years later, he opened a production plant in Detroit with the help of copper millionaire S. L. Smith, but things didn't go well. After two struggling years in the business, Olds decided that the public wanted a simpler kind of car. His answer was a little one-cylinder runabout he called the "curved dash" Olds, and it was an immediate success. Not only was it simple, but the unique curved dash was an exciting element of style that made the car sell like mad. In 1901, the car's first year of production, 425 were produced. Four years later, production reached 6,500. The "curved dash" Olds was America's first mass-produced automobile, and it set a standard of styling that the industry has followed ever since.

---

# George B. Selden

George B. Selden never got his hands dirty working on cars, but it could be argued that he built America's first gas-powered automobile, on paper at least. A New York patent lawyer by profession, Selden had a little engineering training and did some inventing in his spare time. He got the idea of building an automobile in 1876, when he saw a two-cycle gasoline engine invented by George Brayton at the Philadelphia Exposition. Selden had his own Brayton-type engine built that same year and designed, on paper, a road carriage on which to mount it.

Whether for lack of money or lack of interest, Selden didn't build his motor carriage, but he did have the foresight to apply for a patent in 1879, at which point he sat back and waited. He waited sixteen years, keeping the patent alive with frequent amendments until 1895, when he deemed it time to let the patent come through and start collecting royalties.

Selden's patent was, for the most part, airtight, but many of the new car makers refused to honor it and went ahead making and selling their cars. The most famous such patent breaker was Henry Ford, who fought Selden in the courts from 1903 to 1911, when a U.S. Court of Appeals ruled in favor of Ford. But by that time Selden's patent had only one year to go, and he had already collected considerable royalties.

If only for the satisfaction of his many detractors, Selden finally did build a working model of his original automobile in 1905. Or, it should be said, he hired a mechanic to build it. He thus invented the automobile in America, was in the auto business for thirty-five years, yet never lifted a wrench.

# Alexander Winton

Every auto pioneer benefited from an auto race at one time or another, but none learned to exploit the publicity potentials of auto racing as did Alexander Winton, a Scot who came to the U.S. at the age of twenty, opened a bicycle shop in Cleveland, Ohio, and built his first automobile there in 1896. Although his first car was not as evolved as some others being made around the same time, Winton had an unflagging desire to get into the auto business that gave him an edge over other makers.

A year after making his first auto, Winton built two phaeton-type horseless carriages and actually sold one to a local Clevelander. It seemed a good start, but the car's buyer returned a few days later and demanded his money back. This was just the first of a string of unhappy customers who plagued Winton, slowing his sales. Finally, in an effort to dispell rumors that his cars were unreliable, Winton drove one 800 miles from Cleveland to New York in the amazing time of ten days. Suddenly, he was back in business.

Riding a wave of nationwide fame, Winton began entering his cars in every road and track race, every hill-climbing and endurance contest he could find. For the next few years, Winton's famous "Bullit" racing machines set speed records. In 1900, a Winton became the first automobile to cross the country, making the trip from San Francisco to New York in 81 days. By 1901, the Winton was America's best-selling car and Winton himself was the national track champion. But alas, Winton's success wasn't to last. Other enthusiastic auto makers arrived on the scene, such as Henry Ford, and the competition on which Winton had thrived began to leave him in the shadows. The times, they were changing.

## Henry Ford

Henry Ford is said to have first acquired an interest in mechanics at the age of twelve, when he saw a steam-powered threshing machine on his father's farm in 1875. It was an interest that grew quickly and that eventually led him to become one of America's richest men, as well as the undisputed champion of the American automobile.

Already by his early teens Ford had taught himself to repair watches, a skill that bought him a ticket off the farm to work in a jewelry shop in the city at seventeen. Through his twenties, while working as a mechanic and an engineer for various companies in Detroit, Ford tinkered in his workshop at home. In 1891, an idea occurred to him while he was repairing a stationary four-cycle gasoline engine in a Detroit bottling factory. He hadn't paid much attention to gasoline engines before, but suddenly it was clear to him that such an engine could be adapted to power a vehicle. He went home, told his wife, and set to work.

At 2:00 A.M. on June 4, 1896, Ford's first automobile

was ready for its maiden test. As he began to push the car out to the street, the mechanical genius noticed a minor oversight: He had built the car wider than his shop door. Not about to let that stop him, he promptly removed part of the shop wall with a sledgehammer and rolled the auto onto the cobblestones. With his wife and a friend to help, Ford spent the next two hours fiddling with the car until it ran to his satisfaction. It did, and from that point forward, Ford's sole aim was to make and sell automobiles.

Success didn't come overnight. In fact, it took three years before Ford could get anybody interested in the idea of investing in a motor car company. When he finally did get some investors interested and started a company, it failed. He immediately formed a second auto company, but it too failed. In 1903, Ford established a third automobile company. It is called the Ford Motor Company.

Ford started the company while at the crest of new fame brought to him by a racing car he built called the 999. Although he had no interest in racing, he had hoped that success in the new sport would attract potential financiers. He hired the famous bicycle racer Barney Oldfield to drive the 999. Oldfield had never driven a car before, but he won his first race by an overwhelming margin, beating all the best drivers of the day. Suddenly, both Oldfield and Ford were famous.

The Ford Motor Company produced about 200 automobiles in its first year of production, 1903. The first car was a 2-cylinder runabout that sold for $850. In 1904, Ford built another racer in which he set a world record for the mile—39.4 seconds. Again, publicity surged and sales soared. In 1905, Ford sold more than 1000 of his new Model Bs, at $2000 each. The ball was rolling.

Publicity for the company soon came to a positive peak with Ford's huge legal battle over the auto patent held by George Selden, a New York patent attorney. The public was vastly in support of Ford, who was looked on as a small business man being victimized by the vultures of Wall Street. Under the constant attention of the press, Ford business thrived. In 1907, the company finished with a profit of $1 million.

The following year, 1908, Ford sacked his high-priced 6-cylinder model to concentrate production on his new brain-child, the Model T. New, yes, but years of planning and effort had gone into this car, and it was soon seen to be Ford's masterpiece. It was not attractive, powerful, or luxurious. Some people even called it downright ugly. But it was wonderfully straightforward, reliable, and cheap, and it quickly proved to be exactly what America needed.

In 1927, when Ford stopped production on the Model T, 15 million had been made and well over half the cars then on America's roads were Model Ts. Henry Ford may not have invented the automobile in America, but he had made it accessible. With his perfected techniques of mass production, he had put America at the forefront of a new age, and with his automobiles, he had transformed the country and how its people lived. Perhaps it could be said that Henry Ford invented a new America.

## Hiram Maxim

Hiram Percy Maxim was part of a line of inventors. His father had gained a certain amount of fame as the inventor of the Maxim gun and the explosive known as maximite. In 1892, Hiram himself went to work on a gasoline-powered engine with which to power a self-propelled road vehicle, as he called it. Considering the crudeness of his beginning experiments, it is remarkable that Maxim had a running automobile in only three years.

For example, Maxim started by putting one or two drops of gasoline in a heavy cartridge case, shaking them around to create a vapor, then dropping a match in. The explosion would send the cartridge bouncing around the shop. A slight refinement of this procedure led to Maxim's first carburetor—a gas-soaked rag that would drip gas into the combustion chamber at a fairly constant rate. The rag was an important part of Maxim's developing automobile: When it became clear that his engine would need to be cooled from the constant explosions, Maxim surrounded the cylinder with water-soaked rags. Then, when the loud popping became too noisy, Maxim made a crude muffler—yes, out of rags.

# Charles Kettering

Long before the automobile had gotten beyond being an oddity on the streets of America, engineers and inventors had begun working on a variety of new gadgets and devices that would make the horseless carriage a more practical and convenient form of transportation.

The speedometer, shock absorbers, the foot accelerator, the electric horn, tire chains, demountable rims, and electric headlights were all invented during the first ten years of the century. There soon followed the windshield wiper (hand-operated), the rear-view mirror, brakelights, and one invention by a man named Charles Kettering that was worth more than all the other inventions put together—the self-starter.

People had tried for years to solve the problem of the manual ("crank") starter and had come forth with a variety of contrivances. Their so-called self-starters operated by springs, metal linkages, compressed air or gas, but the problem was that none of them worked. Until Kettering's invention in 1911—by which time most electrical engineers had concluded the electric self-starter was a practical impossibility.

Kettering's self-starter was actually fairly similar to one of his earlier inventions—an electric motor for opening a cash register drawer, which he had invented while working for the National Cash Register Company. He had already considered the possibility of an automobile self-starter when he heard that the Cadillac auto company was dissatisfied with its auto's ignition system. Kettering put his idea to Henry Leland, the head of Cadillac, and Leland bought it. Two years later, the Kettering self-starter was perfected. It made its debut on the 1912 Cadillac.

It could easily be argued that Kettering did as much for women's liberation as he did for the automobile. Before the self-starter, driving an automobile had been for men only. Most women just didn't have the muscle to turn the manual crank and thus were dependent on men to at least start their cars. Suddenly, the self-starter made them free.

But perhaps more important, Kettering's invention changed the automobile from an unreliable and even dangerous contraption only for the mechanically minded to a reliable and practical vehicle for anyone who could turn a key.

# It's All in the Family

Ned Jordan, who became known for his impressive "Playboy" car and its unusual ad campaigns, was sales manager at the Thomas B. Jeffery Company in 1915, when the company premiered the Chesterfield series. It was Jordan who named the new car line.

Fred S. Duesenberg, who inadvertently lent his name to the slang word *duesy*, began working at the Thomas B. Jeffery Company in 1903 as a car tester.

Walter P. Chrysler worked for the American Locomotive Company, General Motors, and Willys-Overland before producing his own car.

John N. Willys was a car dealer for the Detroit Automobile Company (which became the Cadillac Auomobile Company) before he launched his own vehicles.

C. Harold Wills worked for Henry Ford in the early days of automobile history. He went on to produce the Wills-St. Claire.

Henry Leland, Robert C. Faulconer, and Horace E. Dodge, familiar names in automobile lore, were once employed by Ransom E. Olds and had a hand in creating the original curved dash Oldsmobile.

Charles Nash also clocked in for another auto maker, William C. Durant, before he built his first auto.

Louis Chevrolet raced Buicks prior to presiding over the sports cars of the Frontenac Motor Company

John Z. DeLorean, whose car was featured in the 1985 movie *Back to the Future*, worked for many years at General Motors and Pontiac.

## Opportunity Knocked

Impatience has been the cause of many a missed opportunity. Take, for example, the case of Barney Oldfield, who gained sudden great fame in his partnership with Henry Ford, driving Ford's pioneer racing machine, the 999. It was a partnership of mutual advantage, generating priceless publicity from the start, but Ford needed money to make money, and although he had promised the great driver a piece of the action once his dream company was perfected, Oldfield didn't have the time to wait around. Instead, Barney signed a contract with Alexander Winton.

Many years later, Ford, while on a business trip to the West Coast, decided to look up Oldfield and pay him a visit. He found him down on Spring Street, in downtown Los Angeles, where Barney had opened a saloon after his retirement from racing.

"Well, Barney," said the multimillionaire in greeting his former partner. "You made me, and I made you."

"Yes," Oldfield admitted. "But I did a damn sight better job of it than you did."

# Americans Adapt

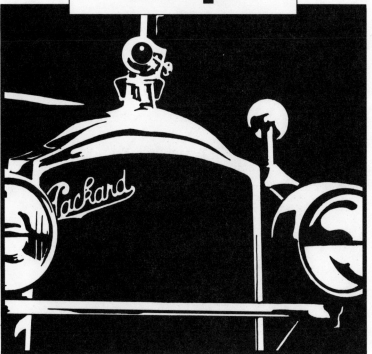

# This Horseless Carriage Came with a Horse

Frightening horses was for many early automobile operators one of motoring's greatest worries. Most car builders of the period could see no solution to the problem, but one man thought he had the answer. Uriah Smith, founder of the Horsey Horseless Carriage Company of Battle Creek, Michigan, developed a motor car that came with a life-size wooden horse's head attached to its front. The fake head was supposed to disguise the car with a visage friendly to oncoming animals, but no explanation was given as to how horses would reconcile the noise of the car's engine.

# But Do They Give Out Diplomas?

In 1900, in the small town of Chesterfield, New Hampshire, the only family with an automobile was that of Thomas Derr. "Out of respect for the horses and their drivers," Derr later wrote, "we sent word around town that we would not take the car out on Sundays. Some farsighted farmers, however, thought that it would be better to get their horses accustomed to the car, as there would probably be more to come—so we held a course of training. Someone usually sat in the car so that the horse could see its resemblance to a buggy. As a horse approached, he was given sugar to calm his nerves. When he reached the point where he could stand seeing steam blown out of the engine without trying to run away, he was considered a graduate and 'broken in.' "

## A Leg Up on Horse Sense

Steam-car specialist Thomas Derr well understood the horse's early fear of the automobile. He recalls: "As a professor of psychology has said, the mental reaction of a horse when he first saw a 'horseless carriage' must have been similar to what ours would be if we should see a pair of pants walking down the street by themselves without anyone inside."

## Red Flag Ahead

An article in *Ainslee's Magazine* (vol. 7, no. 213) in 1901 printed this amusing legal note:

> A judge of the Supreme Court in New York has held that the owners of steam automobiles should be required to send a runner with a red flag ahead of the vehicle to warn other wayfarers.

# A Cure for Parched Wheels

During the summer, California's Imperial Valley is one of the hottest, driest places on earth. Routine daytime temperatures hover around 110°F, and at night the mercury often rolls back only a few degrees, or not at all. This unusual climate had some interesting effects on early-model automobiles, which manufacturers hadn't anticipated, but which innovative mechanics of the area put to rights in their own special way.

The early Ford Model T, for example, had wooden wheels that would lose all their moisture to the parched air; the spokes would shrink up and rattle noisily in their sockets as the car rolled along. Clark Smith, a clever mechanic in the valley's capital of El Centro during the 1920s, had a remedy: "Whenever we'd have a car jacked up to work on it, we'd take off the wheels, tie a rope to them and throw them in the river. When the work was done, we'd pull the wheels out and they'd be tight as a drum. Then we'd have silent wheels again—for a week or two, anyhow."

# Don'ts for Tire Owners

The following list, published by the Automobile Club of America in the late twenties, tells motorists how to baby their cars' tires and gives an indication of the troubles involved in early auto care.

**Do not** apply brakes so hard as to skid the wheels; this is what tears tires to pieces.

**Do not** round corners at top speed; remember that in turning corners, particularly when a car is loaded, there is great strain on the tires. Figure this out.

**Do not** let the tires rub the curb; the steering knuckle may become bent and the tires badly worn on one side.

**Do not** let in the clutch so that the car starts with a jerk; this tears the tread of the tires and is apt to part the rubber from the fabric.

**Do not** permit water to creep between the tires and the rims; the fabric will be rotted from the water and from the rust that will form on the rims.

**Do not** run at speed over roads that have rocks or crushed stone on the surface; give the tires a chance to respond to the inequalities of the road.

**Do not** drive in streetcar tracks; they will cut the tires on the outside edge in a short time.

**Do not** take railroad tracks, bridges, crosswalks, etc., head on and at speed; take them at an angle and slow down, so as to avoid pinching the inner tube.

**Do not** *guess* the tires have enough air; put on a gauge and *know* it.

**Do not** go out without an extra casing, two extra tubes, a repair kit, a pump, and an air bottle. The last-named is one of the blessings of motoring; it has taken away half the troubles.

**Do not** become hasty or excited in making a tire repair; time will always be saved by taking things as they come and making the best of them.

**Do not** permit a car to rest on a deflated tire; it will soon cut the casing and pinch the tube.

**Do not** fail to use talcum or soapstone in the casing when making a change or when putting in a new tube; it prevents friction and adhesion.

## Silence Is Olden

One of the beautiful things about the steam car was the utter silence with which its engine ran. Compared to the bombastic chatter of the gasoline auto, the steamer rolled along at a whisper. One of the Stanley brothers, of Stanley Steamer fame, had an experience that illustrates the point.

While on a trip to the South, when the automobile was still a novelty, Mr. Stanley took an opportunity to convince a prospective buyer of his car's fine qualities. The two men jumped in the car and headed down a hill to a bridge with a toll gate. The gatekeeper was sound asleep and Mr. Stanley briefly toyed with the idea of quietly passing the keeper without paying the toll. Instead, he woke the keeper and asked, "Have you seen our horse anywhere?" The man glanced over their horseless carriage and groggily replied, "I'm sorry, sir. I haven't seen your horse, but if there is anything I can do to help you find him, I'd be glad to."

## Charles the Chauffeur

Charles, the chauffeur, and milady, Juliet,
The dashingest pair of the autoist set,
All primed for adventure, are out for a spiel,
On this fine country road, in their automobile.

As they dash down the pike, without quaver or hitch,
The farmers in front of them take to the ditch.
And the cohorts that follow are trailing afar
Like the Netherby clan after young Lochinvar.

After climbing a long grassy slope, at the top
The pulsing machine has been brought to a stop,

For the silt of the air and microbic flies
Have reddened the lids of milady's bright eyes.

And Charles, at the signal, has stopped the machine
And passed back the bottle containing Murine.
So milady leans back, and looks up at the sky
As the magic "two-drops" are dropped into each eye.

Now again they are off, at a forty-mile pace,
With vision restored and new zest in the race;
And woe betide him who opposes their gait,
For he's booked for a serious tussle with fate.

The automobile, by some unwritten code,
Has won, in fee simple, all rights to the road;
And quite as true title indisputably, lies,
To the trite, but true saying, "Murine cures eyes."

—from a 1907 Murine advertisement

## Of Playboys and Ponies

The era of Gatsby, of Prohibition, of rakish young men
and daring young women—these years of elegance and
hedonistic good times have never been equaled. The
wealthy sported new costumes, they frolicked brazenly,
and they adopted the automobile as a toy of adventure
and panache. The advertisements below got to the heart
of the sale. No facts and figures. No words of market-

able dependability or remarkable utility—just style. Pure style.

## SOMEWHERE WEST OF LARAMIE

Somewhere west of Laramie there's a broncho-busting, steer-roping girl who knows what I'm talking about.

She can tell what a sassy pony, that's a cross between greased lightning and the place where it hits, can do with eleven hundred pounds of steel and action when he's going high, wide and handsome.

The truth is—the Playboy was built for her.

Built for the lass whose face is brown with the sun when the day is done of revel and romp and race.

She loves the cross of the wild and the tame.

There's a savor of links about that car—of laughter and light—a hint of old loves—and saddle and quirt. It's a brawny thing—yet a graceful thing for the sweep o' the Avenue.

Step into the Playboy when the hour grows dull with things gone dead and stale.

Then start for the land of real living with the spirit of the lass who rides, lean and rangy, into the red horizon of a Wyoming twilight.

—Jordan, 1923

Or try its earlier incarnation:

## THE JORDAN PLAYBOY

A spirited companion for a wonderful girl and a wonderful boy. It's a shame to call it a roadster. So full of this brawny, graceful thing of the vigor of boyhood and morning.

It carries two passengers with a cockpit—swanky seat behind.

It revels along with the wandering wind and roars

like a Caproni biplane. It's a car for a man's man—that's certain.

Or for a girl who loves the out-of-doors.

It's true—there's some of the tang of that rare old English ale that was brewed from the smiles of youth and of old boxing-gloves.

How did we happen to think of it?

Why a girl who can swim and paddle and shoot described it to a boy who loves the roar of the cut-out.

We built one and slipped away from the quiet zone.

And stepped on it.

And the dogs barked.

And boys stopped to cheer.

And people we passed stopped and looked back.

And we were boys again.

The Playboy will be built in limited numbers—frankly because we love to do it.

—Jordan, 1922

This even earlier approach just began to hint at the change in advertising tactics:

## MAIBOHM

*Whizzing Speed!* peaceful idling—it makes a fellow's blood tingle to look at a car like this and feel that it belongs to him—unleashed it will roar nose to nose with an express train; checked it will glide along composedly behind a mule team; a spirited car, ravenous to devour the miles: a gentle, sooothing car, mild as a kitten: coachwork with the symmetry of a Rembrandt: springs that lull where others crash: upholstery from a cow's back—the lightest good six ever made.

—Maibohm, 1920

# The Long and Winding Road

One of the great obstacles to the development of the automobile in America was the sorry condition of her roads. In France, Napoleon had left behind him a fine network of paved interurban highways. But American roads actually got worse in the nineteenth century, with ferryboats and railroads putting the few good toll roads out of business. At the turn of the twentieth century, the United States had a mere 160 miles of hard-surfaced road. Most of the country's 2 million miles of roads were narrow dirt wagon paths that turned to impassable quagmires in wet weather.

"As to roads," wrote one J. F. Miller, who with his wife made one of the first long-distance tours by car in 1904, "it may be said that there are no good ones in America. This country scarcely knows the meaning of the word."

Not until the establishment of the United States Office of Public Roads in 1904 did the picture begin to brighten. State-aid plans began to get federal funds for their roads. In 1913, the auto makers started a nationwide campaign to construct a coast-to-coast paved road they called the Lincoln Highway. Their organization, the Lincoln Highway Association, was headed by Henry Joy, president of the Packard Motor Car Company, who had tried to cross the U.S. only to find areas where the road was nothing more than "two ruts across the prairie." Enthusiasm for the project ran high, with hundreds of state and local politicians competing to have the highway run through their community. As a result, the road zigged and zagged to connect stretches paved by local enthusiasts from New York through Philadelphia and Pittsburgh; across northern Ohio, Indiana, and Illinois; through Iowa and Nebraska to cross the Continental Divide in southern Wyoming, and then down through Salt Lake City, Utah, to northern Nevada; finally, it crossed the Sierra Nevada via the Donner Pass into California. When completed, the Lincoln Highway ran 3389 miles from Times Square, New York City, to Lincoln Park, San Francisco.

In 1925, Louis B. Miller and his mechanic, C. I. Hansen, crossed the country on the Lincoln Highway in a new Wills-St. Claire Six Roadster. Their time of 4 days and 7 hours between New York and San Francisco broke all previous coast-to-coast records by car and took only 6 hours longer than the fastest train. In 1900, the coast-to-coast trip had required 81 days.

By 1928, the Lincoln Highway Association considered the route completed and celebrated by having Boy Scouts across the country erect concrete markers along the highway. By then a surge of road improvement had taken place around the nation so that some 60,000 miles of paved roads were available to motorists. From then on, there was no looking back—except through the rear-view mirror, of course.

# Early Road Laws Make Today's Look Easy

Drivers who think today's road laws are too strict ought to be transported back to certain rural parts of Pennsylvania around the turn of the century. At that time, a group of farmers calling themselves the Farmers' Anti-Automobile Society got together and set up some "rules" for local car owners:

1. Automobiles traveling on country roads at night must send up a rocket every mile, then wait ten minutes for the road to clear. The driver may then proceed, with caution, blowing his horn and shooting off Roman candles, as before.
2. If the driver of an automobile sees a team of horses approaching he is to stop, pulling over to one side of the road, and cover his machine with a blanket or dust cover which is painted or colored to blend into the scenery, and thus render the machine less noticeable.
3. In case a horse is unwilling to pass an automobile on the road, the driver of the car must take the machine apart as rapidly as possible and conceal the parts in the bushes.

On the Sabbath, anti-car group members, as well as all self-respecting members of the community, were encouraged to "chase automobiles, shouting and shooting at drivers, and threatening them with arrest."

---

# Wherefore the Coffee Break

The evidence is strong that we owe the invention of that glorious American institution—the coffee break—to the automobile industry. Yes, the practice is said to have begun at the American Rolls-Royce factory in Springfield, Massachusetts, sometime between 1910 and 1920.

With a rapidly growing number of employees at the plant and still no cafeteria, Rolls-Royce executives got an idea: An office boy was given the job of serving coffee to the employees—once in the morning and once in the afternoon.

The coffee break had not yet taken on the socializing connotation it has today. The office boy would serve each worker at his or her station, and work carried on almost without interruption.

Another thing about that early coffee break was its stricter definition. You didn't drink your pleasure at the period. You drank coffee. A few imported Englishmen at the Springfield plant voiced a preference for tea as the practice took hold, but their requests for an option were denied, and they eventually adjusted to the stronger beverage.

# One Dissatisfied Customer

Alexander Winton, founder of the Winton Motor Carriage Company, which manufactured the first automobile in America on a regular production schedule, didn't exactly write the book on customer service; rather, he had his own methods. When a dissatisfied customer hitched his Winton to a pair of horses and paraded it through downtown Cleveland with a sign reading, "This is the only way you can drive a Winton," the auto manufacturer hired a wagon loaded with a mule to follow it with a placard bearing the message, "This is the only animal unable to drive a Winton."

# Every Mechanical Failure

Despite claims to the contrary, the 1908 E-M-F did have its problems. And although many early-day motorists swore by their E-M-Fs, a number of them took advantage of the automobile's good name. "Every Mechanical Failure" and "Every Morning Fixit" were only two less-than-discreet nicknames for this car backed by some of the most noted authorities of cardom.

# Adaptability Was Its Specialty

The Ford Model T, introduced in 1908, was probably the simplest car ever built. Because of its simplicity, it also quickly became the most adapted, converted, modified, and specialized car in auto history. The T originally sold for $290 without extras, but most proud owners felt it necessary to add one or more of the available non-Ford extras—dashing items such as rubber hood silencers, tool chests, tire-patching kits, clamp-on dashlights, and fixable flower vases.

From there, ideas for the T's use got ever more elaborate and practical. For example, for a small price a farmer could buy a set of two steel tractor wheels manufactured to fit the Ford axle. To use his car in the fields, he had only to remove the standard rear wheels, put on the tractor wheels, and hitch up his plow, planter, harrow, disc, or hay rake.

The car was also used as a portable power plant on the farm. The farmer drove into the woods, jacked up a rear wheel, removed the tire, and ran a belt from the wheel to his buzz saw to cut cordwood for the kitchen stove. People of all kinds, not just farmers, invented new uses for the car. It was used to pump water, generate electricity, grind feed for livestock, operate sheep shears, corn shredders, butter churns, and even sausage grinders.

During the 1920s, one company developed a special

undercarriage that turned the Model T into what the firm called the Snowmobile. The car's front wheels were moved to the rear, and each set of double wheels was fitted with steel caterpillar treads. Steel sled runners were attached to the front axle, and the snowmobile was ready to go. It was used by farmers and woodsmen in the deep snows of the north country.

# You've Come a Long Way . . .

"Any Woman Can Start Your Car"
—The Star Starter Company
1911 advertisement

"The chosen car of men of affairs, as well as the favorite conveyance of Her Highness, the American woman."
—Woods Electric
1910 advertisement

"It is not surprising that the automobile should be popular with women. Few women are experienced drivers, and as a rule they avoid the responsibility of managing a horse. . . . The horseless carriage is more to their liking, inasmuch as they have only to learn how to handle a convenient lever to ride where they will, without any attendant whatever, and with perfect safety."
—*Woman's Home Companion*
January 1900, Volume 27

"If You *Really Want* Your Wife to Drive," began a Chandler advertisement, she can learn by using the unique Traffic Transmission and avoid clashing gears or failing to make a smooth speed change. "Let her learn that its operation is so simple and easy that she can drive coolly through the thickest traffic and take dangerously steep hills without the slightest worry."

—Chandler
1924 advertisement

Packard changed its slogan in 1950, from "Ask the man who owns one!" to "Ask the woman who owns one!" The word *woman* appeared penned-in over the scratched out word *man*. An example of the body of the ad follows: 13,210 miles in three months, through 28 states, Canada, and Mexico. That was my introduction to Packard Ultramatic Drive . . . and every mile of it, from the highest mountains to the busiest city streets, was sheer delight! "I operate 400 acres of farm land, and some apartment properties, so I drive a lot for business as well as for pleasure—and I can assure you that a Packard, with Ultramatic Drive, is the ideal car for a woman!"

The 1955 Dodge Custom Royal LaFemme came complete with matching rain cape, boots, umbrella, and purse.

Modern times bring us the Chrysler Laser Turbo XE, the car "for the woman of the '80s." The company press release continues: "No longer just for the Big Man on Campus or the guy cruising down Van Nuys Boulevard, the 1984 Chrysler Laser Turbo XE denotes the power and authority that women have acquired over the past decade."

# Yankee Ingenuity Goes into the Early Hot Rod

The hot rods of the 1940s weren't the sleek, scientifically engineered machines of modern-day drag racing, but nobody can say they weren't put together with a certain amount of backyard ingenuity. For example, the record-holding speedster of its type in 1948 consisted of a chassis and running gear from a Ford roadster, a Mercury engine, and a body built from the wing tank of a P-38 fighter plane. It looked like a submarine sandwich on wheels, but managed to squeeze out 149.75 M.P.H. on the California desert flats.

# Early Don'ts for Drivers

The following "Don'ts" by Mr. Dave H. Morris, an early president of the Automobile Club of America and member of the Committee on Public Safety, are well worth heeding:

1. Don't disobey the rules of the road.—Remember to keep to the right and pass on the left.

2. Don't forget that pedestrians have the same rights as vehicles at street crossings.—Remember that vehicles do not have the right of way at street crossings.
3. Don't forget that your rate of speed should never exceed the legal rate, whatever it may be.—Remember, when local conditions require, to adopt even a lower rate of speed than the legal rate.
4. Don't get "rattled."—Remember that it is the "other fellow" who always loses his head in a crisis.
5. Don't insist upon your rights.—Remember that the "other fellow" may not know your rights, and an insistence on your part is bound to result in an accident.
6. Don't argue with trolley-cars, express-wagons, brewery-trucks, or other heavy bodies found in the public thoroughfare.—Remember that the drivers of these powerful vehicles generally operate on the theory that might is right.
7. Don't expect women and children to get out of your way.—Remember that many women and children don't know how to avoid danger.
8. Don't run any unnecessary risks.—Remember that while the automobile is flexible, powerful, and easily operated, you may make a slip.
9. Don't drink.—Remember that nine-tenths of the accidents occur to automobiles driven by intoxicated chauffeurs.
10. Don't sneak away in case of an accident.—Remember that the true gentleman chauffeur, although he may not be responsible for the misfortune, stands his ground.
11. Don't fail to be a gentleman under any provocation.—Remember that the Golden Rule practiced on the road will save you no end of trouble, expense, and worry.

# State of the Art of the Previously Owned

Buying a used car isn't every American's automotive dream, but a lot of us do it anyway. How many? How much do we spend? On which cars? Where? These are a few of the questions answered in the following list, compiled from a story in the June 1985 issue of *Motor Trend* magazine. The facts herein, many of them culled from a study done by the Hertz rental car company, give a fairly complete picture of current American habits in buying used cars.

1. In 1984, approximately 18 million used cars were bought in America, about twice as many as were bought new.
2. Nineteen eighty-four's average used car cost about $4900. Average new car that year—$9113.
3. The typical used car bought in 1984 was almost 5 years old and had almost 50,000 miles on it. These figures stand out significantly against the same statistics for 1979, when the typical used car bought was not quite 3 years old and had just less than 30,000 miles.
4. The typical passenger car of the 1980s will have 2.8 owners during its lifetime.
5. Forty-five percent of all automobiles survive through their tenth birthday, but only 5 percent live to be fifteen.

6. About half of all used cars bought in America in 1984 were bought from new-car dealers. Thirty-five percent were sold through private parties, and about half of those transactions were between acquaintances. Less than 15 percent of used cars went by way of used-car dealers.
7. On the average, used-car buyers were younger than new-car buyers, and their average family income was about $10,000 less.
8. The following are the accessories most used-car buyers would forego in order to keep costs down: 83 percent would opt to do without vinyl roofs; 80 percent would eliminate power windows; 52 percent would drop cosmetic trim; 35 percent would delete air conditioning; and 28 percent would settle for a stick shift instead of an automatic transmission.
9. Half of used-car buyers paid cash in 1984, while less than one-third of new-car buyers paid cash.

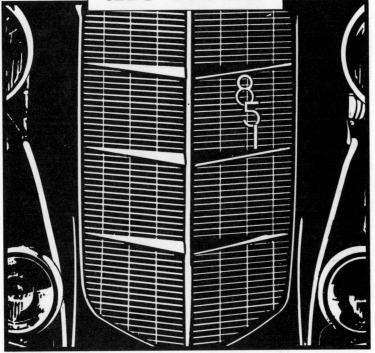

# Kings of
# the Road

# America's First Auto Race

America's first official automobile race took place in Chicago on Thanksgiving Day, November 28, 1895—a day after one of the year's worst storms had dumped a foot of snow on the city. A slight warming trend on race day slowly turned the new snow to near-impassable semifrozen soup, and what had been intended as a serious contest of speed became a comical crawl through the slush.

Eleven cars entered the fifty-mile race, but only six were able to start, and only two finished. As they pulled away from the starting line, at intervals, it wasn't long before each of the six entries had problems. The first starter, Frank Duryea, got only fifteen minutes out before his car broke down. The second car, driven by Frederick Haas, quickly got bogged down in snow, started again, then quit once and for all. The third starter, Jerry O'Conner, got off to a good start, early passing the stalled Duryea, but ended up having the worst luck of the pack. O'Conner smashed into three different carriages on his way, ultimately snapping four wheel spokes, bending his steering wheel, and finally sputtering out altogether.

Duryea got started again and began making steady headway, at roughly 8 miles per hour. The fourth and fifth starters were electric cars, which had not planned ahead to have their batteries recharged and which never had a chance of finishing. A German car driven by Oscar Mueller started last, an hour after Duryea.

More than ten hours after starting, Frank Duryea, co-builder of America's first gas car, crossed the finish line. Stops, breakdowns, and wrong turns included, Duryea averaged 6.66 miles per hour in the race. One hour thirty-five minutes later, Mueller pulled in to finish second, and last.

# Oldfield Gets First One-Minute Mile

The one-minute mile was a great speed barrier for American auto racers around the turn of the century. It was narrowly missed in 1901, when A. L. Riker, driving his Riker Electric Racer, covered the distance in 63 seconds. It was another two years before the legendary Barney Oldfield finally broke the barrier in Henry Ford's 999. Early in 1903, Oldfield went through the mile in 55.8 seconds, or 64.516 M.P.H. Later that year Oldfield bettered that time.

# World Automobile Speed Records

The majority of world speed records have been set on American soil—first, between 1903 and 1930, at Ormond-Daytona Beach, Florida, then on the salt flats of Utah and California.

| YEAR | DRIVER/CAR | AVERAGE M.P.H. |
|------|------------|----------------|
| 1898 | Chasseloup-Laubat/Jeantaud | 24.3 |
| 1899 | Jenatzy/Jenatzy | 40.9 |
| 1902 | Serpollet/Serpollet | 46.6 |
| 1903 | Duray/Gobron-Brillie | 52.6 |
| 1903 | Henry Ford/Ford 999 | 91.4 |
| 1904 | W. K. Vanderbilt/Mercedes | 92.4 |
| 1905 | Arthur MacDonald/Napier | 104.6 |
| 1906 | Frank Marriott/Stanley Steamer | 127.7 |
| 1910 | Barney Oldfield/Benz | 131.7 |
| 1911 | Bob Burman/Benz | 141.7 |
| 1919 | Ralph DePalma/Packard | 149.9 |
| 1920 | Tommy Milton/Duesenberg | 156.1 |
| 1926 | J. G. Parry-Thomas/Thomas Special | 168.1 |
| 1926 | J. G. Parry-Thomas/Thomas Special | 170.6 |
| 1927 | Capt. M. Campbell/Napier-Campbell | 174.2 |
| 1927 | Maj. H. O. D. Segrave/Sunbeam | 203.8 |

KINGS OF THE ROAD

| YEAR | DRIVER/CAR | AVERAGE M.P.H. |
|------|-----------|----------------|
| 1928 | Capt. M. Campbell/Napier-Campbell | 206.9 |
| 1928 | Ray Keech/White Triplex | 207.6 |
| 1929 | Maj. H. O. D. Segrave/Irving-Napier | 231.5 |
| 1931 | Sir Malcolm Campbell/Napier-Campbell | 246.1 |
| 1932 | Sir Malcolm Campbell/Napier-Campbell | 253.9 |
| 1933 | Sir Malcolm Campbell/Napier-Campbell | 174.2 |
| 1935 | Sir Malcolm Campbell/Bluebird | 276.8 |
| 1935 | Sir Malcolm Campbell/Bluebird | 301.1 |
| 1937 | Capt. G. E. T. Eyston/Thunderbolt | 311.4 |
| 1938 | Capt. G. E. T. Eyston/Thunderbolt | 345.5 |
| 1938 | John Cobb/Railton | 350.2 |
| 1938 | Capt. G. E. T. Eyston/Thunderbolt | 357.5 |
| 1939 | John Cobb/Railton | 368.9 |
| 1947 | John Cobb/Railton Mobile Special | 394.2 |
| 1963 | Craig Breedlove/Spirit of America | 407.45 |
| 1964 | Tom Green/Wingfoot Express | 413.20 |
| 1964 | Art Arfons/Green Monster | 434.02 |
| 1964 | Craig Breedlove/Spirit of America | 468.719 |
| 1964 | Craig Breedlove/Spirit of America | 526.277 |
| 1964 | Art Arfons/Green Monster | 536.71 |
| 1965 | Craig Breedlove/Spirit of America Sonic I | 555.27 |
| 1965 | Art Arfons/Green Monster | 576.553 |
| 1965 | Craig Breedlove/Spirit of America Sonic I | 600.601 |
| 1970 | Gary Gablich/Blue Flame | 622.407 |
| 1983 | Richard Noble/Thrust II | 633.468 |

# U.S. Auto Club National Champions

| | | | |
|---|---|---|---|
| 1902 | Harry Harkness | 1927 | Peter DePaolo |
| 1903 | Barney Oldfield | 1928–29 | Louis Meyer |
| 1904 | George Heath | 1930 | Billy Arnold |
| 1905 | Victor Hemery | 1931 | Louis Schneider |
| 1906 | Joe Tracy | 1932 | Bob Carey |
| 1907 | Eddie Bald | 1933 | Louis Meyer |
| 1908 | Louis Strang | 1934 | Bill Cummings |
| 1909 | George Robertson | 1935 | Kelly Petillo |
| 1910 | Ray Harroun | 1936 | Mauri Rose |
| 1911 | Ralph Mulford | 1937 | Wilbur Shaw |
| 1912 | Ralph DePalma | 1938 | Floyd Roberts |
| 1913 | Earl Cooper | 1939 | Wilbur Shaw |
| 1914 | Ralph DePalma | 1940–41 | Rex Mays |
| 1915 | Earl Cooper | 1940–46 | Ted Horn |
| 1916 | Dario Resta | 1949 | Johnnie Parsons |
| 1917 | Earl Cooper | 1950 | Henry Banks |
| 1918 | Ralph Mulford | 1951 | Tony Bettenhausen |
| 1919 | Howard Wilcox | 1952 | Chuck Stevenson |
| 1920 | Gaston Chevrolet | 1953 | Sam Hanks |
| 1921 | Tommy Milton | 1954 | Jimmy Bryan |
| 1922 | James Murphy | 1955 | Bob Sweikert |
| 1923 | Eddie Hearne | 1956–57 | Jimmy Bryan |
| 1924 | James Murphy | 1958 | Tony Bettenhausen |
| 1925 | Peter DePaolo | 1959 | Rodger Ward |
| 1926 | Harry Hartz | 1960–61 | A. J. Foyt |

| | | | | |
|---|---|---|---|---|
| 1962 | Rodger Ward | 1974 | Bobby Unser |
| 1963–64 | A. J. Foyt | 1975 | A. J. Foyt |
| 1965–66 | Mario Andretti | 1976 | Gordon Johncock |
| 1967 | A. J. Foyt | 1977–78 | Tom Sneva |
| 1968 | Bobby Unser | 1979 | A. J. Foyt |
| 1969 | Mario Andretti | 1980 | Johnny Rutherford |
| 1970 | Al Unser | 1981–82 | George Snider |
| 1971–72 | Joe Leonard | 1983 | Tom Sneva |
| 1973 | Roger McCluskey | 1984 | Rick Mears |

# Barney Oldfield

The history of auto racing is scattered with the names of famous drivers—heroes of speed—but none stands out like the name of the great Barney Oldfield. Although he never won the Indianapolis Memorial Day Classic and was never credited as national champion by the AAA, Oldfield dominated the sport of auto racing like no one before or since. During his eighteen-year career in the sport, the famous cigar-chomper outraced the best drivers from around the world, on dirt oval tracks, beach straightaways, and the open road of long-distance cross-country races. To an entire generation, Barney Oldfield was the undisputed king of racing.

Oldfield had started out racing bicycles. He entered his first race at sixteen, in 1894, and soon began winning regularly. He continued racing bicycles as a paid amateur until 1902, when Henry Ford hired him as a mechanic for his new racer, the 999.

Oldfield watched Ford and his partner Tom Cooper lose a few races before convincing them to let him try.

His first time behind the wheel of the 999 (which was also his first time behind the wheel of an automobile), at a five-mile race at Grosse Point track, Oldfield demolished the field in a spectacular display of raw, unharnessed speed. He simply pulled out the throttle to full speed and left it there, turns and all. At the finish he was a half-mile ahead of the pack, which included Alexander Winton in his famous Winton Bullet, then thought to be the fastest car anywhere.

The race quickly made Oldfield famous, but he didn't rest on his laurels. He beat Winton again on December 1, 1902. Then, on Memorial Day, 1903, he drove the 999 to a world record time for the mile—1 minute, 1⅗ seconds. Within months he had broken this record and established another world record for five miles while beating French champion Frank LaRoche.

Oldfield soon parted ways with the Ford 999 gang and started driving for Winton. The change of cars didn't phase him: On November 22, 1903, he drove the Winton to another world mile record—54⅘ seconds. The next time he broke his mile record was in international competition, on the sand flats at Daytona Beach. He defeated such European stalwarts as William Vanderbilt and Henry Bowden and clocked a time of 43 seconds flat.

Part of what made Oldfield such a memorable champion was his brash, reckless character. Off the race track, he had a reputation for being a barroom brawler. Professionally he was cocky, defiant, and often in trouble with racing authorities. (The AAA suspended him from racing once in 1910.) But he was the best. He knew it, and people loved him for it.

Only three years after first driving an automobile, Oldfield had broken more of his own world records than all other records combined. Or look at it this way: By the time Oldfield had firmly established himself as the most successful and popular race car driver of all time, the American automobile was barely ten years old. In 1920, Barney turned in his lead foot and retired from racing.

# Stanley Steamer Sets Two-Mile Record

Between 1903 and 1906, record times for the mile went from 59½ seconds to about 36 seconds. All records went to gas-powered cars, then a sudden change occurred. In January 1906, at an international competition in Ormond, Florida, a specially designed Stanley Steamer driven by Fred Marriott blew the socks off gas-engine proponents by going through *two* miles in less than a minute (59⅗ seconds) for a world speed record of 127.66 miles per hour. It was by far the fastest car in the world—and it was a steamer!

At that same competition, the screamin' steamer set four other world records: one kilometer—18⅖ seconds; one mile—28⅕ seconds; one mile in competition—31⅕ seconds; and five miles—2:47. The Stanley held the two-mile record for more than four years.

## National Association for Stock Car Auto Racing (NASCAR) Grand National Champions

| | | | |
|---|---|---|---|
| 1949 | Red Byron | 1965 | Ned Jarrett |
| 1950 | Bill Rexford | 1966 | David Pearson |
| 1951 | Herb Thomas | 1967 | Richard Petty |
| 1952 | Tim Flock | 1968–69 | David Pearson |
| 1953 | Herb Thomas | 1970 | Bobby Isaac |
| 1954 | Lee Petty | 1971–72 | Richard Petty |
| 1955 | Tim Flock | 1973 | Benny Parsons |
| 1956–57 | Buck Baker | 1974–75 | Richard Petty |
| 1958–59 | Lee Petty | 1976–78 | Cale Yarborough |
| 1960 | Rex White | 1979 | Richard Petty |
| 1961 | Ned Jarrett | 1980 | Dale Earnhardt |
| 1962–63 | Joe Weatherly | 1981–82 | Darrell Waltrip |
| 1964 | Richard Petty | 1983 | Bobby Allison |

## Sundown on the Steamer

If it is true, as most automobile experts believe, that early car racing was largely responsible for the sudden and consistent improvements and technological advances of the commercial auto industry, then perhaps the following story explains why the steam car became extinct.

In 1907, the year after the famous Stanley Steamer racer stunned the world with its two-mile-a-minute speed record, the Stanley brothers returned to the Dewar's Cup at Ormond Beach, Florida, with a much-improved model. They knew no gas-powered car could touch them, and they were confident they could break their year-old record.

The poor condition of the beach held off the first day of the cup races, but then a good northeasterly wind smoothed out the surface and they were ready to begin. Fred Marriott, the same driver who broke the world record for the Stanleys in 1906, gave the new car a test run on which it went through the mile in an easy 29½ seconds, or 122 M.P.H. He noticed one bad spot on the beach, but he was eager to try for a new record and the crowd cheered him on.

With a 9-mile headstart and the boiler pressure built to an explosive 1300 pounds, Marriott set the machine in motion. By the time he crossed the starting line, the car was traveling at a speed never before seen—roughly 180 M.P.H., or 3 miles per minute. Then, still accelerating, he suddenly hit the bad spot and the car went flying. It flew for at least 100 feet, turned slightly as it did, and finally came down with a mighty crash, which tore the boiler out and sent it rolling down the beach several hundred feet. When the Stanley brothers reached the scene, Marriott was unconscious. He had several broken ribs, a nasty gash on his head, and one eye was hanging out of the socket.

Luckily, there was a doctor on hand and Marriott actually recovered full use of the eye and his health. Nevertheless, the Stanley brothers then and there decided never again to risk the life of a man for speed. They never raced their steamers again.

# I Think I Can,
# I Think I Can . . .

In early auto years, hill-climbing contests was one popular alternate to the speed race. A car that could climb a steep hill was a highly regarded machine; and its driver was lauded too, since a car's showing often depended on its driver's ability to extract every last foot-pound of energy from his vehicle—by shedding weight at the right time, or any number of other devices. This is evidenced by a typical scoring system for hill-climbing contests, which rated horsepower and ingenuity as follows:

1. Very good
2. Nicely
3. Steadily
4. Well
5. Easily
6. Tacked up (swerved from one side of road to other)
7. Shed passengers to ease or help push
8. Stuck
9. Shed passengers and stuck

# Pikes Peak Hill Climbs

Pikes Peak rises 14,110 feet from sea level, about half the altitude of Mount Everest. Although its height is impressive, it is not even among the tallest twenty-five mountains in Colorado. It is, however, the site of the annual Pikes Peak hill climb, a race that has been run every year from 1916 to the present, except 1917–1919, 1935, and 1942–1945.

The first "Race to the Clouds" was engineered by Penrose to publicize his new toll road. Three classes of vehicle scaled the heights that day: race cars, stock cars, and motorcycles. Drivers in the first race included Eddie Rickenbacker in a Maxwell, Barney Oldfield in a Delage, and Ralph Mulford in a Hudson; none of these veteran racers won. The Penrose Trophy went to an unknown, Rea Lentz, who drove a Romano Special.

It was no easy feat to reach the top. Zebulon Montgomery Pike, who lent his name to the peak, wrote in his journal on Thanksgiving Day: "It was as high again as what we had ascended, and it would have taken a whole day's march to arrive at its base, when I believe no human being could have ascended to its pinical [sic]." Bobby Unser, who, along with his other famous family members, gained his fame at Pikes Peak said: "I ran into a cloud bank there once, and it scared the livin' hell out of me."

The future of the race is debatable. More and more

national resources, including Pikes Peak, are coming under the scrutiny of environmentalists and government officials. The race doesn't damage the environment as much as the spectators do.

# Pace Cars of the Indianapolis 500

| YEAR | PACE CAR | DRIVER |
| --- | --- | --- |
| 1911 | Stoddard Dayton | Carl G. Fisher |
| 1912 | Stutz | Carl G. Fisher |
| 1913 | Stoddard Dayton | Carl G. Fisher |
| 1914 | Stoddard Dayton | Carl G. Fisher |
| 1915 | Packard 6 | Carl G. Fisher |
| 1916 | Premier 6 | Frank E. Smith |
| 1919 | Packard V–12 (called Twin Six) | Col. J. G. Vincent |
| 1920 | Marmon 6 (Model 34) | Barney Oldfield |
| 1921 | H.C.S. 6 | Harry C. Stutz |
| 1922 | National V–12 | Barney Oldfield |
| 1923 | Duesenberg | Fred S. Duesenberg |
| 1924 | Cole V–8 | Lew Pettijohn |
| 1925 | Rickenbacker 8 | Capt. E. V. Rickenbacker |
| 1926 | Chrysler Imperial 80 | Louis Chevrolet |
| 1927 | LaSalle V–8 | "Big Boy" Rader |
| 1928 | Marmon 8 (Model 78) | Joe Dawson |
| 1929 | Studebaker | George Hunt |
| 1930 | Cord 8 (Lycoming Engine) | E. L. Cord |

| YEAR | PACE CAR | DRIVER |
|------|----------|--------|
| 1931 | Cadillac | "Big Boy" Rader |
| 1932 | Lincoln | Edsel Ford |
| 1933 | Chrysler Imperial (Phaeton) | Byron Foy |
| 1934 | LaSalle | "Big Boy" Rader |
| 1935 | Ford V–8 | Harry Mack |
| 1936 | Packard | Tommy Milton |
| 1937 | LaSalle | Ralph DePalma |
| 1938 | Hudson 112 | Stuart Baits |
| 1939 | Buick | Charles Chayne |
| 1940 | Studebaker | Harry Hartz |
| 1941 | Chrysler Newport (Phaeton) | A. B. Couture |
| 1946 | Lincoln V–12 | Henry Ford II |
| 1947 | Nash Ambassador | George W. Mason |
| 1948 | Chevrolet | Wilbur Shaw |
| 1949 | Oldsmobile | Wilbur Shaw |
| 1950 | Mercury | Benson Ford |
| 1951 | Chrysler V–8 | Dave Wallace |
| 1952 | Studebaker | P. O. Peterson |
| 1953 | Ford | William C. Ford |
| 1954 | Dodge | William C. Newburg |
| 1955 | Chevrolet | T. H. Keating |
| 1956 | DeSoto | L. I. Woolson |
| 1957 | Mercury | F. C. Reith |
| 1958 | Pontiac | Sam Hanks |
| 1959 | Buick | Sam Hanks |
| 1960 | Oldsmobile | Sam Hanks |
| 1961 | Ford Thunderbird | Sam Hanks |
| 1962 | Studebaker | Sam Hanks |
| 1963 | Chrysler | Sam Hanks |
| 1964 | Ford Mustang | Benson Ford |
| 1965 | Plymouth Sports Fury | P. M. Buckminster |

| YEAR | PACE CAR | DRIVER |
|------|----------|--------|
| 1966 | Mercury Comet Cyclone GT | Benson Ford |
| 1967 | Chevrolet Camaro | Mauri Rose |
| 1968 | Ford Fairlane Torino | William C. Ford |
| 1969 | Chevrolet Camaro | Jim Rathmann |
| 1970 | Oldsmobile 4-4-2 | Rodger Ward |
| 1971 | Dodge Challenger | Eldon Palmer |
| 1972 | Hurst-Olds | Jim Rathmann |
| 1973 | Cadillac Eldorado | Jim Rathmann |
| 1974 | Hurst-Olds | Jim Rathmann |
| 1975 | Buick V-8 | James Garner |
| 1976 | Turbocharged Buick V-6 | Marty Robins |
| 1977 | Oldsmobile Delta 88 | James Garner |
| 1978 | Chevrolet Corvette | Jim Rathmann |
| 1979 | Ford Mustang | Jackie Stewart |
| 1980 | Pontiac Turbo-Trans Am | Johnnie Parsons |
| 1981 | Buick Regal V-6 | Duke Nalon |
| 1982 | Camaro Z28 | Jim Rathmann |
| 1983 | Buick Riviera Convertible | Duke Nalon |
| 1984 | Pontiac Fiero | John Callies |
| 1985 | Oldsmobile Calais | James Garner |

# Winners of the Indianapolis 500-Mile Race

| YEAR | DRIVER | ENGINE | CYLINDERS | AVERAGE M.P.H. |
|------|--------|--------|-----------|----------------|
| 1911 | Ray Harroun | Marmon Wasp | 6 | 74.69 |
| 1912 | Joe Dawson | National | 4 | 78.72 |
| 1913 | Jules Goux | Peugeot | 4 | 75.933 |
| 1914 | Rene Thomas | Delage | 4 | 82.47 |
| 1915 | Ralph DePalma | Mercedes | 4 | 89.84 |
| 1916 | Dario Resta | Peugeot | 4 | 84.00[1] |
| 1919 | Howard Wilcox | Peugeot | 4 | 88.05 |
| 1920 | Gaston Chevrolet | Monroe | 4 | 88.62 |
| 1921 | Tommy Milton | Frontenac | 4 | 89.62 |
| 1922 | Jimmy Murphy | Miller | 8 | 94.48 |
| 1923 | Tommy Milton | Miller | 8 | 90.95 |
| 1924 | L. L. Corum/J. Boyer | Duesenberg | 8 | 98.23 |
| 1925 | Peter DePaolo | Duesenberg | 8 | 101.13 |
| 1926 | Frank Lockhart | Miller | 8 | 95.904[2] |
| 1927 | George Souders | Duesenberg | 8 | 97.545 |
| 1928 | Louis Meyer | Miller | 8 | 99.482 |
| 1929 | Ray Keech | Miller | 8 | 97.585 |
| 1930 | Billy Arnold | Miller | 8 | 100.448 |
| 1931 | Louis Schneider | Miller | 8 | 96.629 |
| 1932 | Fred Frame | Miller | 8 | 104.144 |
| 1933 | Louis Meyer | Miller | 8 | 104.162 |
| 1934 | William Cummings | Offenhauser | 4 | 104.863 |
| 1935 | Kelly Petillo | Offenhauser | 4 | 106.240 |
| 1936 | Louis Meyer | Offenhauser | 4 | 109.069 |
| 1937 | Wilbur Shaw | Offenhauser | 4 | 113.580 |
| 1938 | Floyd Roberts | Offenhauser | 4 | 117.200 |

| YEAR | DRIVER | ENGINE | CYLINDERS | AVERAGE M.P.H. |
|------|--------|--------|-----------|----------------|
| 1939 | Wilbur Shaw | Maserati | 8 | 115.035 |
| 1940 | Wilbur Shaw | Maserati | 8 | 114.277 |
| 1941 | F. Davis/M. Rose | Offenhauser | 4 | 115.117 |
| 1946 | George Robson | Thorne/Sparks | 6 | 114.820 |
| 1947 | Mauri Rose | Offenhauser | 4 | 116.338 |
| 1948 | Mauri Rose | Offenhauser | 4 | 119.814 |
| 1949 | Bill Holland | Offenhauser | 4 | 121.320 |
| 1950 | Johnnie Parsons | Offenhauser | 4 | 124.002[3] |
| 1951 | Lee Wallard | Offenhauser | 4 | 126.244 |
| 1952 | Troy Ruttman | Offenhauser | 4 | 128.922 |
| 1953 | Bill Vukovich | Offenhauser | 4 | 128.740 |
| 1954 | Bill Vukovich | Offenhauser | 4 | 130.840 |
| 1955 | Bob Sweikert | Offenhauser | 4 | 128.209 |
| 1956 | Pat Flaherty | Offenhauser | 4 | 128.490 |
| 1957 | Sam Hanks | Offenhauser | 4 | 135.601 |
| 1958 | Jim Bryan | Offenhauser | 4 | 133.791 |
| 1959 | Rodger Ward | Offenhauser | 4 | 135.857 |
| 1960 | Jim Rathmann | Offenhauser | 4 | 138.767 |
| 1961 | A. J. Foyt | Offenhauser | 4 | 139.130 |
| 1962 | Rodger Ward | Offenhauser | 4 | 140.293 |
| 1963 | Parnelli Jones | Offenhauser | 4 | 143.137 |
| 1964 | A. J. Foyt | Offenhauser | 4 | 147.350 |
| 1965 | Jimmy Clark | Ford | 8 | 150.686 |
| 1966 | Graham Hill | Ford | 8 | 144.317 |
| 1967 | A. J. Foyt | Ford | 8 | 151.207 |
| 1968 | Bobby Unser | Offenhauser | 4 | 152.882 |
| 1969 | Mario Andretti | Hawk-Ford | 8 | 156.867 |
| 1970 | Al Unser | Colt-Ford | 8 | 155.749 |
| 1971 | Al Unser | Colt-Ford | 8 | 157.735 |
| 1972 | Mark Donohue | Offenhauser | 4 | 162.962[4] |
| 1973 | Gordon Johncock | Offenhauser | 4 | 159.036 |
| 1974 | Johnny Rutherford | Offenhauser | 4 | 158.589 |
| 1975 | Bobby Unser | Meyer-Drake | 4 | 149.213[5] |
| 1976 | Johnny Rutherford | Drake-Offenhauser | 4 | 148.725[6] |
| 1977 | A. J. Foyt | Coyote-Foyt | 4 | 161.331 |
| 1978 | Al Unser | Lola-Cosworth | 8 | 161.363 |
| 1979 | Rick Mears | Penske-Cosworth | 8 | 158.889 |
| 1980 | Johnny Rutherford | Pennzoil Chaparral | 8 | 142.862 |

**KINGS OF THE ROAD**

| YEAR | DRIVER | ENGINE | CYLINDERS | AVERAGE M.P.H. |
|------|--------|--------|-----------|----------------|
| 1981 | Bobby Unser | Eagle–Offenhauser | 4 | 139.029 |
| 1982 | Gordon Johncock | Wildcat–Cosworth | 8 | 162.029 |
| 1983 | Tom Sneva | March–Cosworth | 8 | 162.117 |
| 1984 | Rick Mears | March–Cosworth | 8 | 162.962 |

Races shortened to these distances because of rain:
[1]300 mi.  [2]400 mi.  [3]345 mi.  [4]332.5 mi.  [5]435 mi.  [6]255 mi.

# New Cross-Country Speed Record Set—17.6 M.P.H.!!!

Alexander Winton, president of the Winton Motor Carriage Manufacturing Company, might have moved slowly by today's standards, but he was a speed demon of his day. In May 1899, over roads that probably looked more like goat tracks, he established a record average 17.6 miles per hour over a 707.4-mile course between Cleveland and New York City.

Winton and partner/navigator Charles B. Shanks pulled out of Cleveland at 7 A.M. on Monday, May 22, Four days later, with a mere 40 hours and 4 minutes' driving time on the clock, they stopped in front of New York's Astor House. The trip was, however, not without mishap.

After smooth sailing on the easy roads between Cleveland and Buffalo, the going got tough. Eighty miles south of Buffalo, on a road which Winton said would "be discreditable in Middle Africa," they ran up over an embankment and snapped the car's front axle squarely in two. It looked as if the trip was finished, but the resourceful Winton quickly headed off to a telegraph office to send for a new axle. Before long they were moving again.

Country horses frightened by the strange machine were another serious obstacle to Winton's headway. But apart from whatever physical tolls the trip exacted from the two men, the trip was fairly inexpensive: the cost of the gasoline for the entire 707 miles was less than a dollar.

## Electric Wins First "Triple A"

The first race ever sponsored by the Automobile Association of America was a 50-mile contest held on Long Island, New York, in 1901. The winner was A. L. Riker, who drove his Riker Electric Racer an average of 24 miles per hour.

# Sebring 12-Hours Grand Prix Winners

| YEAR | DRIVERS | CAR |
|------|---------|-----|
| 1952 | H. Gray & L. Kulok | Frazer–Nash |
| 1953 | J. Fitch & P. Walters | Cunningham |
| 1954 | S. Moss & W. Lloyd | Osca |
| 1955 | J. M. Hawthorn & P. Walters | Jaguar |
| 1956 | J. M. Fangio & E. Castellotti | Ferrari |
| 1957 | J. M. Fangio & J. Behra | Maserati |
| 1958 | P. Collins & P. Hill | Ferrari |
| 1959 | P. Hill, O. Gendebien, D. Gurney, & C. Daigh | Ferrari |
| 1960 | O. Gendebien & H. Herrmann | Porsche |
| 1961 | P. Hill & O. Gendebien | Ferrari |
| 1962 | J. Bonnier & L. L. Bianchi | Ferrari |
| 1963 | J. Surtees & L. Scarfiotti | Ferrari |
| 1964 | M. Parkes & L. Maglioli | Ferrari |
| 1965 | J. Hall & H. Sharp | Chaparral |
| 1966 | K. Miles & L. Ruby | Ford |
| 1967 | M. Andretti & B. McLaren | Ford |
| 1968 | H. Herrmann & J. Siffert | Porsche |
| 1969 | J. Ickx & J. Oliver | Ford |
| 1970 | M. Andretti, N. Vacarella, & I. Guinti | Ferrari 312 |

| YEAR | DRIVERS | CAR |
|------|---------|-----|
| 1971 | V. Elford & G. Larrouse | Porsche |
| 1972 | M. Andretti & J. Ickx | Ferrari 312P |
| 1973 | P. Gregg, H. Haywood, & D. Helmick | Porsche Carrera |
| 1975 | H. Stuck & A. Moffat | BMW CSL |
| 1976 | A. Holbert & M. Keyser | Porsche Carrera |
| 1977 | G. Dyer & B. Frisselle | Porsche Carrera |
| 1978 | B. Redmann, C. Mendez, & B. Garretson | Porsche Turbo |
| 1979 | B. Akin, R. Woods, & R. McFarlin | Porsche Turbo |
| 1980 | D. Barbour & J. Fitzpatrick | Porsche Turbo |
| 1981 | H. Haywood, A. Holbert, & B. Leven | Porsche Turbo |
| 1982 | J. Paul, Jr. & J. Paul, Sr. | Porsche Turbo |
| 1983 | W. Baker, J. Mullen, & K. Nierop | Porsche 934 |
| 1984 | M. DeNarvaez, H. Heyer, & S. Johanson | Porsche 935 |

# Dreams of Speed Turn Real

Auto racing got an early grip on America. It seemed the car had just learned to walk and already it was running with more speed than most people ever dreamed possible. The thrill and excitement of this new and ever-increasing speed infected thousands, and in no time auto racing was part of our lives. America's greatest car race got its start back in the sport's early days and is still with us today—the Indianapolis 500.

The Indy didn't start as a 500-mile race. In fact, the first race ever run on the grand new oval was only 5 miles. That was the opener in a three-day series of races that took place when the track first opened its doors to the public on August 19, 1909. It was an immense success, having attracted some 80,000 people and netted a handsome profit of $50,000. However, five people died during the event as a result of the dangerously rutted dirt track, and safer conditions were promised before the staging of another race.

Nearly two years passed and many improvements were made before the inaugural 500-miler. The two and a half mile-track had been paved with 3.2 million bricks, and officials and drivers alike proclaimed its safety. On May 30, 1911, the starting gun fired for the first 500-mile Memorial Day "International Sweepstakes."

Forty starters jumped out of the blocks with a deafening roar that sent the crowd of 90,000 gleefully to its feet. It was an unpredictable free-for-all through the first 60 miles: the lead changed five times, and one car lost a wheel and swerved into the side wall, killing the mechanic. But things finally settled down with David Bruce-Brown in an Italian-made Fiat at the head of the pack.

At 160 miles Ray Harroun, piloting his Marmon Wasp, No. 32, snatched the lead and from that point never relinquished it. Nevertheless, the excitement didn't stop. While there were no further serious accidents or injuries, many minor ones spiced the competition throughout. At one point a nasty pile-up on the home stretch left one mechanic with a broken leg; at another, a car went out of control in the pitstops, sending a loose bolt into the face of a spectator and an injured mechanic to the hospital.

More than six and a half hours after the gun, a weak and wobbly Harroun pulled into the winner's circle—$10,000 richer.

Twenty-two of the 40 starting cars finished the competition, which the press called "a great race and a grand struggle." Since that first race, countless other great moments in the history of car racing have taken place in subsequent Indys, repeatedly proving it one of the world's great car races.

# New York to Paris— The Hard Way

Wild and crazy endeavors were anything but uncommon during the infancy of the motor carriage. Heck, before 1905 almost *any* automotive endeavor outside of a jaunt around town or a few miles into the country for a picnic was considered adventurous—almost certain to include difficulty and exasperation, if not injury. As soon as enthusiastic motorists had conquered their local environs, they reached out fearlessly to tackle more daring, dangerous destinations; they fairly raced to take on obstacles of increasingly absurd proportions. By 1908, this excited attitude led to what undoubtedly still reigns as automobiling's most preposterous event—the around-the-world New York-to-Paris race.

The idea was cooked up by a Paris newspaper, *Le Matin*, which had staged the only slightly less outrageous Peking-to-Paris race the previous year. That race was won by Prince Scipione Borghese, who tried to dissuade people from future races of the sort, pointing out that his accomplishment had had very little to do with motoring, since three-quarters of the trip was made without roads of any kind. But the Paris newspaper turned a deaf ear to Borghese and went ahead with plans for the great contest.

The initial route crossed the continent from New York to Seattle, where contestants would head north through Canada and into Alaska as far as Dawson City. From there they were to head west across the Yukon to the Bering Straits, where they would commence to drive *across the ice* into Siberia, continuing southwest to a point just short of the Manchurian frontier, where they would connect with the Peking-Paris route. By the time they got to Paris, the contestants would have traveled some 17,000 miles and circled the planet, not including the Atlantic crossing.

Almost as soon as it was proposed, the route was rejected. In 1908, most of Alaska and Siberia was still unexplored and almost undoubtedly impenetrable, particularly in winter, when the race was scheduled so as to ensure ice thick enough to hold the cars. Also, this route didn't take into account the fact that no car had ever crossed America on so northerly a route, let alone during the winter. Finally, it was agreed that the cars would go to San Francisco instead of Seattle. There they would get on a ship to cross the Bering Sea to Siberia, where they'd continue according to the original plan.

When the starting gun fired over Times Square on February 12, 1908, a total of six cars were at the line: three French, one German, one Italian, and one American. The entrants were a motley bunch, with an extraordinary variety of cars to match. One car carried a pair of skis that could be attached to the front end for use in deep snow. Another car was equipped with a mast and sail for added speed when the winds were favorable. Yet another, the French Motobloc, was fitted with several large cabinets that carried tools, spare tires, and a large supply of champagne for celebrating special occasions.

The first day of the race, only the American Thomas Flyer, the French DeDion, and the Italian Zust achieved the scheduled destination of Hudson, 116 miles out. The Motobloc called it a day in Peekskill, New York, 70 miles from Manhattan. There, as night descended after several hours spent digging their auto out of a snow drift, the Motobloc's crew discovered they'd forgotten to bring food. They had only champagne.

A few of the New York-to-Paris participants had also raced in the previous year's Peking-to-Paris event. On reaching San Francisco after the grueling trek across the American continent, these contestants readily concurred: crossing China last year had been a piece of cake. Just three days after leaving New York, Lieutenant Koeppen, commander of the German Protos, pronounced dourly, "Siberia will be a picnic after this."

Four of the six starters eventually made it to San Francisco, all of them roughly five weeks behind schedule. Only one, the Thomas Flyer, shunned the boat ride and attempted to continue up the coast through British Columbia and into Alaska, but on arriving there, it was immediately clear that the unexplored territory was utterly impassable. Realizing their mistake, the Flyer crew then quickly caught a boat to Japan like the rest.

A month later, when the race got under way again at the Russian port of Vladivostok, it was anything but a picnic. At one point in crossing the continent, the Thomas Flyer's crew was forced to remove its car's wooden fenders to use as huge mud sandals. The Flyer had reached Siberia in last place, but it had gained quickly and was helped when the German car was penalized 15 days for not stopping to cross Japan by car, going straight to China by ship instead. The French DeDion pooped out somewhere along the vast Russian steppes, and it became a 3-car race to the finish.

Six months after leaving New York, the Thomas Flyer ground to a final halt outside the Paris offices of *Le Matin*, winner of the first around-the-world car race. Most of *Le Matin*'s staff had already gone home for the evening, but fortunately a group of New Yorkers who had witnessed the race's start were on hand to cheer the American victors. A representative of the sponsoring journal was hastily summoned and finally appeared with the obligatory bottle of champagne. A brief toast was made before the weary winners wandered off to their hotel. The following morning *Le Matin* devoted one-eighth of a column to the epic journey, other Paris papers even less.

The Flyer and its crew got a far more deserving welcome on their return to New York, but even at home the applause was limited to the still-young automobiling set and a weak nationalistic cheer from the public, who were at least happy to have beaten the Europeans. (The Italian Zust was eventually awarded second place, Germany's Protos losing that position due to another penalty.)

Despite the obvious boost the race had given to the American auto industry, American newspapers balked. Wrote one reporter: "A wonderful achievement, but apparently we do not yet need to write the epitaph of the horse."

# Indianapolis Motor Speedway Hall of Fame Personalities

### 1952

Louis Chevrolet
Bert Dingley
Carl G. Fisher
Harvey Firestone, Sr.
Henry Ford

Ray Harroun
Barney Oldfield
Fred J. Wagner
William K. Vanderbilt
T. E. (Pop) Myers

### 1953–54

Bob Burman
Earl Cooper
Ralph DePalma
Tommy Milton

Ralph Mulford
Dario Resta
Eddie Rickenbacker

### 1962

Fred Duesenberg

### 1963

Peter DePaolo
Augie Duesenberg
Harry Hartz
Rex Mays
Louis Meyer

Harry Miller
Wilbur Shaw
Harry C. Stutz
Howard Wilcox

## 1964

James A. Allison
Gaston Chevrolet
Eddie Hearne

Ted Horn
Jimmy Murphy

## 1965

Frank Lockhart

## 1967

Tony Hulman

Mauri Rose

## 1968

Tony Bettenhausen

Jean Marcenac

## 1969

Lou Moore

Harry (Cotton) Henning

## 1970

Ralph Hepburn

Bill Cummings

## 1972

Bill Vukovich

## 1973

Jimmy Bryan

## 1975

George Bignotti

## 1976

Cliff Bergere                    Joe Dawson

## 1977

Billy Arnold

## 1978

A. J. Foyt, Jr.                  Leo Goossen

## 1980

David Bruce-Brown               George Robertson
J. Walter Christie

## 1981

Johnny Aitken                   Jimmy Snyder
E. G. (Cannonball) Baker        Rodger Ward
Sam Hanks                       A. J. Watson
Art Pillsbury

## 1982

Harry Grant                     Lewis Strang
Fred Offenhauser

## 1983

Gil Anderson                    Dennis (Duke) Nalon
Cliff Durant                    Myron Stevens
Harlan Fengler                  Ed Winfield
Frank Kurtis

**1984**

Clint Brawner
Fred Frame

Ray Keech

**1985**

Henry Banks
Joe Boyer

Parnelli Jones
Floyd Roberts

# A Driving Personality

Keith Johnsgard, a psychologist interested in road racing, came up with a race-driver personality profile for *Road and Track* magazine in 1976. The results, below, are an approximate translation of a chart that plots the average scores of thirty world-class racers. The chart offers two alternatives (i.e., high sex drive and low sex drive); the plotted points displayed how salient each quality was, rating them from 0 to 100. The translation just lists the overall results.

High abstract intelligence
High achievement needs
Assertive, aggressive
Unsympathetic, uncaring
Disorganized, unpredictable
Tough-minded, realistic
Leader, dominant
Dislikes criticism, praise
High sex drive

Independent, autonomous
Guilt free, irresponsible
Self-sufficient
Detached, reserved, cool
Exhibitionistic
Happy-go-lucky
Expedient, makes own rules
Seeks change, new experiences
Insensitive to others
Little need for people

# The Martyrs

Think what you will of the racing man,
　Say what you like as well,
Call him a "nut with a heavy foot,"
　Crazed by the Speed Imp's spell.
Brand him as greedy for purse and fame,
　Jest at his playlike toil—
Riding hell-bent in a roaring bowl,
　Blackened with grime and oil.

Give him a cheer or scoff at his kind,
　But when he leaves the track—
A broken thing 'mid a wreck of steel
　To ride through vales of black—
Be square to him and just ask yourself
　As fairly as you can:
"Would I give as much as he has spent
　For the good of my fellow man?"

Remember, too, as you roll along
   Security's Highway,
You owe a debt to this "speed-mad fool,"
   A debt you'll never pay.
For he's taken tires, bolts, and rods
   To prove them false or true,
And his O.K. is your guaranty
   That you'll ride safely through.

—J. C. Burton

# True Love

# The Magical New Powers of the Automobile

Many early proponents of the automobile made extraordinary claims about the variety of ills curable by the introduction of this new machine, but few were as far-reaching as the beliefs of one Irvin Cobb. In a 1923 issue of *Motor*, Cobb puts forth the idea that World War I might have been avoided if Europe had had an abundance of inexpensive automobiles. He reasoned that the ill-will between different peoples would disappear if common men could drive around and see that those of foreign lands were essentially good, peace-loving people like themselves.

Cobb's universal solution for peace: "Give to every people of every land better roads and more automobiles and we shall do away with most of the ill-will that exists among human beings."

# Historical Total Automobile Registrations in the United States

| YEAR (DEC. 31) | AUTOMOBILES |
|:---:|:---:|
| 1980 | 124,435,000 |
| 1975 | 106,077,384 |
| 1970 | 88,775,294 |
| 1965 | 74,909,365 |
| 1960 | 61,419,948 |
| 1955 | 51,960,532 |
| 1950 | 40,190,632 |
| 1945 | 25,694,926 |
| 1940 | 27,372,397 |
| 1935 | 22,494,884 |
| 1930 | 22,972,745 |
| 1925 | 17,493,701 |
| 1920 | 8,131,522 |
| 1915 | 2,332,426 |
| 1910 | 458,377 |
| 1905 | 77,400 |
| 1900 | 8,000 |

(Source: U.S. Federal Highway Administration *Highway Statistics*, 1984 edition)

# The Steamer Performs a Few New Tricks

Eager to demonstrate the superiority of the steam car over the gasoline-powered automobile, early steamer enthusiasts went to great lengths to invent a variety of unique tricks their cars could do.

For example, one steamer lover claimed that any steam-powered automobile would come to its master at a whistle, like a well-behaved dog. This clever stunt was achieved by a bit of delicate timing, as follows: The operator would park his car and let the engine cool down for thirty minutes or so. Then, inconspicuously if possible, he would open the car's throttle slightly. Since with a cooled steamer there is a short delay between opening the throttle and the engine becoming warm enough to move the car again, the operator would have time to walk down the road a bit, turn around, and whistle. If the timing was right, the car would just then begin to move toward its master. Bystanders would be amazed.

Another steam car owner, curious about the epithet of "peanut roaster" commonly attached to steam cars, demonstrated his steamer's value in that capacity during a trip from New York to Boston. Before leaving New York, he bought a package of raw peanuts and placed them on top of the boiler. By the time he reached the Connecticut line, the peanuts were perfectly roasted, and reportedly made a fine finishing touch to his midday meal.

On a different trip, the same driver mixed hot water from his car's boiler with bouillon cubes to make soup. Only later, after downing the soup, did he remember that part of the boiler was made of lead and might have poisoned him. No adverse effects, however, were noted.

On yet another occasion, a steamer owner wagered his car could smoke a pipe and a bystander took him up on the bet. Thereupon, the owner removed the strainer from his car's suction hose (normally used to draw water into the car), placed the stem of a lighted pipe into the hose, opened the suction valve slightly, and the pipe began to glow.

Steam cars have also been used to free clogged house drains, and in at least one city they were used to thaw frozen fire hydrants.

## Eight Great Make-out Cars

*Motor Trend* magazine (Feb. 1973; 25:2) named the following 8 automobiles as the all-time best cars for making out. Each was said to possess unique virtues in accommodating amorous endeavors. Presumably, each of the 8 cars excelled above the rest depending on the endeavor in mind.

1950 Oldsmobile Fastback
1940 Ford Convertible
1957 Chevrolet Hardtop
1948 Mercury Woody
      Wagon
1963 Volkswagen Van
1953 Cadillac Convertible
1949 Mercury
1953 Chevrolet Panel

# The Choices of the Masses

As part of their sociological study of middle America called *Middletown—A Study in American Culture*, sociologists Robert and Helen Lynd analyzed automobile ownership in one mid-size Midwestern city in 1923. Their findings:

- Middletown auto total: 6,221 (approximately 2 cars for each 3 families)
- 54% were late models, made between 1920 and 1923
- 2,578 Fords (41% of total)
- 590 Chevrolets
- 459 Oaklands
- 343 Dodges
- 309 Maxwells
- 295 Buicks
- 264 Studebakers
- 88 Overlands
- 74 Willys-Knights
- 73 Nashes and Interstates
- 65 Durants
- 62 Stars
- 59 Oldsmobiles
- 53 Saxons
- 50 Reos
- Each of the following makes had between 25 and 50 cars: Chalmers, Franklin, Essex, Hudson, Cadillac, Chandler, Monroe, Paige, Haynes, International, Sheridan, and Hupmobile.

- 69 other makes had fewer than 25, including 15 Marmons, 14 Packards, 1 Pierce-Arrow, and 1 Lincoln.
- Total of 97 makes in Middletown.

## Celebrity Cars

Marilyn Monroe owned a hot-pink 1955 convertible Thunderbird.

Elvis Presley's Pantera sold for approximately $2 million in the early 1980s.

Rin-Tin-Tin and his owner, Lee Duncan, chose a 1930 Model U Hudson Touring Sedan as their car.

Mary Pickford, "America's Sweetheart," owned a 1921 Rolls-Royce Salamanca.

Before Captain Eddie Rickenbacker became America's most renowned World War I flying ace and later lent his name to an automobile, he drove an Army-purchased Hudson Super Six.

James Dean's infamous auto in *Rebel Without a Cause* was a Mercury from the 1950s.

Comedian Bob Hope's first car in Hollywood was a 1937 Packard.

John Wayne drove a 1953 Corvette, which is now a part of the Harrah collection.

# Average Expenditure Per New Car in America

| YEAR | AVERAGE AMOUNT |
|------|----------------|
| 1983 | 10,527 |
| 1982 | 9,853 |
| 1981 | 8,929 |
| 1980 | 7,591 |
| 1975 | 4,949 |
| 1970 | 3,542 |
| 1965 | 3,014 |
| 1960 | 2,853 |
| 1955 | 2,506 |
| 1950 | 2,210 |

(Source: "Expenditure Per Car," unpublished data, U.S. Bureau of Economic Analysis, U.S. Department of Commerce)

# In the Presidents' Garages (and Other Presidential Lore)

An automobile served as the ambulance that carried President William McKinley from the site of his assassination to the hospital.

President Theodore Roosevelt rode in an automobile to help promote the invention of the speedometer. The car, at this time, was still not used in official ceremonies.

William H. Taft was the first President to allocate an allowance for transporation and to switch from horse-drawn carriages to automobiles.

The first four official presidential cars were a white seven-passenger touring steam auto, two Pierce-Arrows, and a Baker Victoria phaeton.

On December 28, 1923, President Woodrow Wilson received a black Rolls-Royce with orange trim and a small Princeton tiger on the radiator cap. (Black and orange are Princeton's school colors.)

Warren G. Harding broke tradition by riding to his Inauguration in an automobile. It was a Packard Twin Six.

President Calvin Coolidge, whose car was a dark-blue Pierce-Arrow, never allowed his chauffeur to exceed 16 M.P.H.

Franklin D. Roosevelt conducted his first campaign, for state senator, in a brilliant red Maxwell, nick-named the Red Peril.

By the Eisenhower years, the presidential fleet numbered 36 official vehicles. When Kennedy took office, the White House holdings had grown to include 131 cars. President Johnson then decreased the number of official automobiles to 20.

Richard M. Nixon's personal car was a 1968 "Stretch" Lincoln limousine, complete with custom-built armored safety features.

## The Modern Blacksmith

Under a costly canopy
  The village blacksmith sits;
Before him is a touring car
  Broken to little bits,
And the owner, and the chauffeur, too,
  Have almost lost their wits.

The village blacksmith smiles with glee,
  As he lights his fat cigar,
He tells his helpers what to do
  To straighten up the car,
And the owner, and the chauffeur, too,
  Stand humbly where they are.

The village blacksmith puffs his weed
  And smiles a smile of cheer
The while his helpers pump the tires
  And monkey with the gear—
And the owner, and the chauffeur, too,
  Stand reverently near.

The children going home from school
  Look in at the open door;
They like to see him make his bills
  And hear the owners roar,
And the chauffeurs weep as they declare
  They ne'er paid that before.

He goes each morning to the bank
    And salts away his cash;
A high silk hat and long frock coat
    help him to cut a dash—
But the owner, and the chauffeur, too,
    Their teeth all vainly gnash.

The chestnut tree long since has died,
    The smith does not repine;
His humble shop has grown into
    A building big and fine,
And it bears "Garage" above the door
    On a huge electric sign.

*—Chicago Post*

# Five Early Car Songs

1. "In My Merry Oldsmobile"   Vincent Bryan and Gus Edwards
2. "Take Me for a Buggy Ride" Bessie Smith
3. "The Stanley Steamer"   Gloria DeHaven, Mickey Rooney, and Agnes Moorehead
4. "There's Nothing Like a Model 'T' "   Phil Silvers and others
5. "See the U.S.A., in Your Chevrolet"   Dinah Shore

(Credit is attributed to the performer, except for "In My Merry Oldsmobile.")

## Ten Car Songs of the Fifties

1. "Riding in My Car"   Woody Guthrie
2. "Maybelline"   Chuck Berry
3. "Race with the Devil"   Gene Vincent
4. "Brand New Cadillac"   Vince Taylor
5. "Beep Beep"   The Playmates
6. "Hot Rod Race"   Tiny Hill
7. "Drive In Show"   Eddie Cochran
8. "Buick '59"   The Medallions
9. "Drive In"   Richard Hayman
10. "Riding in the Moonlight"   Chester Brunett and Jules Taub

(Credit is attributed to the performer.)

## Ten Car Songs of the Sixties

1. "Hot Rod Lincoln"   Johnny Bond (also Charlie Ryan)
2. "Drive My Car"   The Beatles
3. "Little Deuce Coupe"   The Beach Boys
4. "From a Buick 6"   Bob Dylan
5. "Car Party"   The Sunrays

6. "Hot Rod USA"   The Barracudas
7. "Mustang Sally"   Wilson Pickett
8. "Drag City"   Jan and Dean
9. "Drivin' Wheel"   Little Junior Parker
10. "Ride in Your New Automobile"   Lightnin' Hopkins

(Credit is attributed to the performer.)

# Ten Car Songs of the Seventies

1. "Cadillac Walk"   Mink DeVille
2. "I'm in Love with My Car"   Queen
3. "Hot Wheels"   Albert King
4. "Mercedes-Benz"   Janis Joplin
5. "Cruisin' "   Smokey Robinson
6. "Automobile Blues"   John Prine
7. "Mercury Blues"   Steve Miller Band
8. "Stranded in a Limousine"   Paul Simon.
9. "Lord Mr. Ford"   Jerry Reed
10. "Paradise by the Dashboard Light"   Meatloaf

(Credit is attributed to the performer.)

# Five Car Songs of the Eighties

1. "Pink Cadillac"   Bruce Springsteen
2. "Hot Rod Hearts"   Robbie Dupree
3. "Cars"   Gary Numan
4. "Little Red Corvette"   Prince
5. "Freeway of Love"   Aretha Franklin

(Credit is attributed to the performer.)

# The Milestone Car Society's Milestones

Founded in 1971, the Milestone Car Society celebrates "the great postwar cars, 1945–1970." With a membership growing to 5,000 enthusiasts, the society offers a magazine—*The Mile Post*—that includes information on current nominations, arguments for and against the nominations, classified ads, and local and national news. The nominations are the life blood of the group. A member nominates a car—year span, make, and model—and defends why the automobile should be considered a milestone. The society says that the member must attest to "its relative excellence in at least two of the following areas: styling, engineering, performance, innovation or craftsmanship." A committee of prominent experts then makes or denies the recommendation for approval. The current list of American Milestone Era cars follows.

Apollo  1963–66
Buick Riviera  1949, 1963–70
Buick Skylark  1953–54
Cadillac Eldorado  1953–58, 1967–70
Cadillac Eldorado Brougham  1957–58
Cadillac 60 Special  1948–49
Cadillac 61 Coupe (Fastback)  1948–49
Cadillac 62 Sedanet, Convertible DeVille  1948–49
Chevrolet Bel Air V8 Hardtop & Convertible  1955–57
Chevrolet Camaro SS/RS V8 & Z–28  1967–69
Chevrolet Corvette  1953–70
Chevrolet Nomad  1955–57
Chrysler 300 Letter Series  1955–65
Chrysler Town & Country  1946–50
Continental Mark II  1956–57
Corvair Monza  1960–64
Corvair Monza Spyder  1962–64
Corvair Monza/Corsa  1965–69
Crosley Hotshot/SS  1950–52
Cunningham  1951–55
DeSoto Adventurer  1956–58
Dodge Coronet R/T  1967–70
Dodge Charger R/T & Daytona  1968–70
Excalibur II Series  1965–69
Ford Mustang GT/GTA V–8  1965–67
Ford Mustang Boss 302/Mach 1  1969–70
Ford Crestline Skyliner  1954
Ford Skyliner (Retractable)  1957–59
Ford Crown Vic Skyliner  1955–58

Ford Sportsman   1946–48
Ford Thunderbird   1955–57, 1958–60
Frazer Manhattan   1947–50
Gaylord   1955–57
Hudson (All)   1948–49
Hudson Hornet   1951–54
Imperial   1955–56
Kaiser Darrin 161   1954
Kaiser Deluxe/Deluxe Virginian   1951–52
Kaiser Dragon   1951–53
Kaiser Manhattan   1954–55
Kaiser Vagabond   1949–50
Kiaser Virginian (Hardtop)   1949–50
Lincoln Capri   1952–54
Lincoln Continental   1946–48, 1961–64
Lincoln Continental Convertible   1958–60, 1965–67
Lincoln Continental Custom Limos (Lehman
Peterson)   1961–67
Mercury Cougar XR–7   1967–68
Mercury Sportsman   1946
Mercury Sun Valley   1954–55
Morgan Plus Four   1950–64
Muntz Jet   1950–54
Nash Healey   1951–54
Oldsmobile 88 (Coupe, Convertible, Holiday)   1949–50
Oldsmobile 98 Holiday HT   1949
Oldsmobile Fiesta   1953
Oldsmobile 442   1964–70
Oldsmobile Toronado   1966–67
Packard Caribbean   1953–56
Packard Custom (Clipper & Custom Eight)   1946–50
Packard Pacific/Convertible   1954
Packard Panther Daytona   1954
Packard Patrician/400   1951–56
Plymouth Fury   1956–58
Plymouth Satellite SS & GTX   1965–70

Plymouth Barracuda Formula S    1965–69
Plymouth Roadrunner & Superbird    1968–70
Pontiac Safari    1955–57
Pontiac GTO    1964–69
Shelby 350GT & 500GT    1965–67
Sunbeam Tiger Convertible    1965–67
Studebaker Avanti    1963–64
Studebaker Gran Turismo Hawk    1962–64
Studebaker Starlight Coupe (All)    1947–49
Studebaker Convertible (All)    1947–49
Studebaker Starlight Coupe (Six & V–8)    1953–54
Studebaker Starliner Hardtop (Six & V–8)    1953–54
Studebaker President Speedster    1955
Tucker    1948
Willys Overland Jeepster    1948–51
Woodill Wildfire    1952–58

# The Auto and the Big Apple

New York City is not the most practical place to drive a car, most residents would agree. Public transportation is usually faster, always safer, and even when it's not faster, finding a parking place near your intended destination is usually either prohibitively expensive or just plain impossible. If you don't pay sky-high prices at the parking garage, you ring up an unhealthy total of new gray hairs: either way, you pay.

Still, New Yorkers love their cars as much as anybody. In 1983, 1.5 million private vehicles were registered in New York, which represented a steady increase over the previous ten years, and experts expected the numbers to keep rising. And that number does not include all the autos that pour into Manhattan from outlying areas through the city's tunnels and bridges: On workdays, that figure averaged roughly 45,000 autos daily in 1983, authorities said. Here are some other interesting facts about cars and the Big Apple:

• On the last annual count, for 1984, the streets of New York's five boroughs contained 927,000 potholes.
• Taxi owners and drivers around the city agree that the endurance limit for a cab faced with New York's bad streets and pitiless passengers is 100,000 miles or one year, whichever comes first.
• In recent years, large Chevrolets are the most popular cars in New York, especially with professional drivers. And because there are so many of them, they are also the most popular with thieves, who mostly use them for "chopping," breaking down to use as parts for other Chevys. In November 1984, the New York Police Department Auto Crime Division listed the most frequently stolen cars as follows:

1. 1979 Chevy
2. 1977 Chevy
3. 1978 Chevy
4. 1984 Olds
5. 1980 Chevy

A 1978 Ford is the first non-General Motors car on the list, at number 17. Chrysler comes in at number 26 with a '77 Dodge. Just how popular was the '79 Chevy with New York's thieves? During the month of November, 1979, theft totals for that model were 125.

• 92,000 cars were stolen in New York City in 1983.

# 1984's Most Popular Colors

## FULL-SIZED/INTERMEDIATE CARS

1. Light red-brown
2. White
3. Dark blue
4. Light blue
5. Gray (silver)

## COMPACTS

1. Light red-brown
2. White
3. Light blue
4. Dark blue
5. Red

# Ten Notable Early Car Slogans

1. "Buy a 'Bates' and Keep Your Dates" —Bates, 1905
2. "Ride in a Glide *Then* Decide" —The Glide, 1911
3. "The Car of No Regrets" —Eight Cylinder King, 1915

4. "Not a single experiment embodied in the whole car." —The Reeves "Sextoauto," 1912
5. "No clutch to slip—No gears to strip" —The Gearless Car, Metz "22," 1913
6. "The Car of a Hundred Reasons" —Walter, 1907
7. "The Motor That Motes" —Dragon, 1907
8. "There's a lot of satisfaction in knowing that your car can 'burn up the ground,' if desired, and you don't have to take another car's dust." —The Oakland, 1911
9. "It's as Roomy for Five as It's Chummy for Two" —Anderson Six, 1920
10. "The Car That Made Good in a Day" —Stutz, 1911

# For Philatelists Only

It may come as a surprise to many hobbyists that automobiles and American stamps have a short history of coincidence. Most of the postage stamps that celebrate the motor vehicle come from countries known for the beauty of their stamps: Bhutan, Monaco, San Marino, Yugoslavia. Other countries with distinctive auto issues include Ajman ("Champions of Sport" set highlights some race car drivers), Germany, Hungary, Maldive Islands, Mali, Paraguay, Sharjah, and Umm al Qiwain.

The first car stamp to be issued in the United States shows two men on a car in front of the Capitol building. The 1901 commemorative celebrated the Pan American Exposition.

In 1952, the year of the fiftieth anniversary of the American Automobile Association, the United States issued a series of stamps depicting the cars of 1902.

A four-cent "Wheels of Freedom" stamp was issued on the opening day of the 43rd National Automobile Show, in 1960.

Henry Ford and his Model T graced a 12¢ stamp in 1966, commemorating the pioneer's 105th birthday.

A 1920s touring car appears on the 1970 stamp honoring the women's suffrage movement.

In the early 1980s, a group of prominent citizens from Oyster Bay, New York, and its environs proposed a stamp commemorating the country's early Vanderbilt Cup races, but the stamp was rejected because the race was considered a local event by the postage committee.

The 1980s also brought to the United States a series of stamps that included an electric auto of 1917 (on a 17¢ stamp) among other early vehicles.

The first automobile with a combustion engine—a three-wheeled Benz & Cie vehicle that was manufactured in Mannheim, Germany, in 1886—was celebrated in Germany in 1986 with the issuance of a stamp.

# The Lingo of the Hot Rod Craze

If you were a teenage boy in Southern California during the 1940s, one of your dreams was to drive a hot rod—one of the new modified backyard speed machines made from an old-model car. Hot-rodding at its height seemed ready to overtake the minds of young Americans, and it quickly developed a language all its own: In its June 1946 golden jubilee issue of *Ford Times*, the Ford Motor Company defines the "hot rod lingo" of the era:

- Hot rod, rig, outfit, hot iron—Fast roadster or other stock model automobile worked on by a hop-up
- Hop-up—Person (usually a young fellow) who tinkers with a car to increase its speed
- Gook wagon—Fancy, chromed, noisy, stock car with no speed refinements
- Squirrel—High school-age owner of a sad imitation of genuine hot rod
- Stacks—Exhaust pipes
- Pots, jugs—Carburetors
- Skins, boots—Tires
- Slugs—Pistons
- Drag, peel off, lay a strip—To accelerate rapidly
- Binders—Brakes
- Goat, dog, crutch, crock—(Never a jalopy. This is as unpardonable as referring to a slick chick as a flapper.) Ancient car with no mechanical refinements
- Mill—engine

# More Slogans

"It's a whole new car"
—Dodge Charger, 1975

"The steal of the century"
—Buick Century, 1973

"Building a better way to see the USA"
—Chevrolet, early 70s

"More kicks than a sack full of jack rabbits"
—Corvette, 1962

"What a lot of people have been waiting for"
—Chrysler Fury, 1975

"Dedicated to the free spirit in just about everyone"
—Buick Skyhawk, 1975

"The hot one's even hotter"
—Chevy, 1956

"There's more to it than meets the sky"
—Dodge 600 ES Turbo, 1985

"Any way you measure it, it more than measures up"
—Oldsmobile Calais, 1984

"It's the family car that didn't forget the family"
—Olds Delta 88, 1984

# Love for the Car People Loved to Hate

No matter how bad a certain model or make of car is—how ugly, how poorly designed, how mechanically unsound, no matter how short-lived—there will always be a few people around who love them, if only because everybody else hates them. Some people are just like that: They're attracted to the unpopular.

Strangely, this can't be said of Perry Piper, founder of the Edsel Owners Club of America. Oh, it's true that Piper liked his first Edsel, but not so much that he wanted to start a club around it. That happened later, when he couldn't get *rid* of it.

An Illinois traveling salesman who had long been a loyal Packard driver, Piper finally switched to Ford in 1959, since Packard had stopped making cars. Two years later, when Piper went to trade in his Edsel, nobody wanted it.

The Ford Company had made only 110,847 of the ill-fated autos, and by 1961 they had become such a laughingstock that people were embarrassed to drive them. Some people think the Edsel died because it was big when small cars were growing in popularity. Others attribute its demise to having too many gadgets (it boasted no fewer than 28 accessories never seen before, such as push-button gears and wraparound tail lights).

And then some people thought it was just plain ugly.

"Back then," Piper said, "the dealer would say, 'If you got an Edsel to trade, you keep the car and I'll give you $50.' "

After encountering a few dealers of this type, Piper gave in and bought another car, but he hung on to his Edsel. He grew to love it more, almost as it became more disdained and valueless, and finally Piper determined to find out if he was the only Edsel nut in the world. "I got to thinking," he said, "there must be other people with Edsels out there."

Piper bought ad space in a few magazines, hoping to uncover these like-minded folk. Before long, Piper's local post office was handling 4000 letters a week from Edsel enthusiasts everywhere.

The self-forming group continued to grow until it became the Edsel Owners Club, a 1500-member association that meets regularly to admire each other's autos, discuss state-of-the-art Edseldom, and generally to celebrate the renaissance of their 410-horsepower gas-guzzling dinosaurs.

But while Edsel owners might love and honor their once-scorned ugly ducklings, Edsels would probably still be worthless if it weren't for a chain of events that occurred in 1969, just as Perry Piper was getting his club started. It was then that Piper got a call from Edsel Henry Ford.

At first Piper thought the caller was a crank, but on learning that Edsel Henry Ford was the man's real name and that he was no relation to the auto maker, Piper came to his senses. Quickly assessing the publicity potential of associating a man so named with the Edsel Owners Club, Piper immediately named Edsel Henry Ford president of the club.

True to Piper's guess, it wasn't long before the news

media got wind of the story. Charles Kuralt showed up, as did the *Wall Street Journal*.

Piper says it was the front page *Wall Street Journal* article, which appeared in 1969 on the tenth anniversary of the Edsel's dying gasp, that dispelled the curse of worthlessness from the car. One Edsel owner had told the interviewing reporter, "I wouldn't take $5,000 for my car if I couldn't get another one." When they printed the quote, however, they left off the "if I couldn't get another one." Suddenly the Edsel was worth $5,000.

In 1984, an East Coast Edsel owner is reported to have been offered $30,000 for his car. So it seems Perry Piper, who now owns a fleet of fourteen Edsels, is having the last laugh.

Of the car he once did his best to get rid of, Piper has said: "The Edsel is without question one of the greatest automobiles ever built."

# Unusual Cars
# and Gadgets

# Here Sits the Bride

In the 1960s, '70s, and '80s, getting married in unusual places has been no big thing. Weddings have taken place in hot-air balloons and under the surface of the ocean with Scuba gear on. So the idea of getting hitched in a hot tub doesn't bring you to your feet. But what if the people getting married in a hot tub were also in a car and that car was tooling through the streets of Las Vegas and there were also twenty people present, and there was a bartender serving drinks, too? Well, that's exactly what one couple did in 1984 to claim the world's first mobile hot tub wedding. He wore black swimming trunks and a bow tie, while the bride was in a pure-white one-piece bathing suit with veil and garter. Owned and operated by the Villas Roma Motel and Wedding Chapel in Las Vegas, the 32-foot customized Lincoln limousine was equipped with a musical horn that could play two dozen appropriate wedding themes.

# The Original Easy Rider

In 1911, M. O. Reeves of Columbus, Indiana, began to market "the only easy-riding car in the world"—the Octoauto. It was a conventional car in all respects but one—

the Octoauto had eight wheels. The principle behind this unusual configuration was that of the railroad pullman car, whose many wheels gave it a smooth, shock-resistant ride. "The whole arrangement is very simple and is a shock-absorber beyond the dreams of the neurotic," read one ad for the car. Tires on the Octoauto were said to last eight times as long as tires on ordinary cars. However, despite these remarkable attributes, the Octoauto quickly rolled down the road to oblivion—though no doubt very smoothly.

# An Early Answer to the Call of the Wilds

Quiz time: What was the first rear-engine automobile built expressly for camping?

The Volkswagen Bus? Wrong. It was a car designed and built in 1947 by a Californian named Roy Hunt, a Hollywood cameraman who thought the average automobile wasn't fit for camping and who thus decided to make his own. Hunt's finished camper looked much like other sedans of the period, but it hid many secrets. First, to power his nature wagon, Hunt chose a 4-cylinder, 90-horsepower, air-cooled Franklin engine from a war-surplus airplane, which he placed at the rear. With that out of the way, he had room under the hood of the car for a complete kitchen, including dinette, icebox, sink, GI gas stove, folding table, and dishes. The seats of the car converted into full-length beds, and by unfurling a can-

vas tarp from atop the car's roof, campers were pro-
tected from inclement weather.

As far as is known, Hunt never attempted to mass-
market his ingenius camper. Perhaps he wanted it all to
himself.

# Ten Notable Mid-Century
# Prototypes

(They made fewer than ten.)

| YEAR | CAR | COMPANY | LOCATION |
|------|-----|---------|----------|
| 1948– 50 | Airway | T. P. Hall Engineering Corp. | San Diego, California |
| 1954 | Aurora | Father Alfred A. Juliano | Branford, Connecticut |
| 1946 | Beechcraft Plainsman | Beech Aircraft Co. | Wichita, Kansas |
| 1946 | Darrin | Darrin Motor Car Co. | Los Angeles, California |
| 1949 | Del Mar | Del Mar Motors, Inc. | San Diego, California |
| 1955 | Forerunner | William Flajole | South San Francisco, California |
| 1948 | Gordon | H. Gordon Hansen | San Lorenzo, California |
| 1946 | Stout Project Y | Kaiser-Frazer Corp. | Toledo, Ohio |
| 1961 | Hydramotive | Hydramotive Corp. | Charlotte, North Carolina |

UNUSUAL CARS AND GADGETS

# Early Options and Unusual Features

The Octanator, a water injection system, was advertised: "No longer a military secret."

A tire patch kit was an option for early Ford owners.

Dust guards were attached to the back of an open tonneau to protect back seat passengers from the road's dirt.

In its early days, the rear-view mirror was optional; it didn't become standardized until approximately ten years after it was introduced.

The Wotherspoon Buffet Company offered the Auto Buffet, "a portable box that is strapped to the running board of your car. Can be used as a seat." It kept its contents cold—at 36 degrees—for 15 hours and was electrically lighted.

A ruby safety reflector offered a protective rear guard when tail lights were still unknown.

Fender skirts and bumper guards were common options in the '30s.

In 1935, Chevrolet offered a cigar lighter, a clock, a heater, a radio and antenna, and a license plate frame as options.

The 1954 Nash Ambassador offered "needlepoint upholstery in decorator colors," a precursor to the designer interiors later offered by American Motors.

Candy-striped hubcaps were available for $8.45 a set in 1959.

## Thief Stoppers Old and New

Today's cars have sophisticated electronic sensors that sound a piercing siren when an unauthorized person tampers with the vehicle. Many of them are so sensitive that they will go off if you stop to tie your shoe on their bumper. But anti-theft devices were available back in automotive olden times. All you needed was a piece of wire and an ordinary mouse trap. One wire went from the trap to the horn, the other from the trap to a grounding point on the frame. If a thief tried to move the steering wheel or stepped on the clutch, the mouse trap sprung and the horn sounded a steady blast.

Another thief stopper of autos' early days was a little harder on the criminal. This one consisted of a high tension wire running from the coil up through the car's gear shift. If the thief managed to get the car started, he wouldn't get far. As soon as he touched the gear shift, he got a jolt of electricity that would throw him out of the car.

# To Catch a Thief

Are there any city dwellers out there who aren't familiar with the piercing wail of an auto anti-theft alarm? Probably not. Auto alarms have become as common as sunroofs and bucket seats—so common, in fact, in places like New York City, where an alarm goes off every few minutes or so, that one wonders if it doesn't soon get to be like crying wolf. But in the end the question is, Do they work?

According to security experts in the field, if a professional thief intends to steal a car, no security device—special locks, alarms, fuel or ignition cutoffs, no matter how sophisticated—is going to stop him.

"The thief of today is sophisticated," Stuart Sharenow, president of an automotive anti-theft device manufacturer, told *The New York Times* in 1985. "The pickings are higher and he has new techniques, so if he wants the car badly enough he'll get it."

In 1983, the National Automobile Theft Bureau reported that one in every 46 motor vehicles registered in the United States was either stolen or vandalized. In New York City alone, 92,000 cars were stolen in that year, which is an average of 1764 cars stolen each week, or 252 stolen each day.

But this doesn't mean that security devices are useless, said Sharenow, "because most people who try to steal cars are amateurs." John Runnette, another expert, added that most car thefts are "opportunity thefts."

"Thieves work on a time basis," said Runnette. "All any alarm or cut-off switch can do is slow them down, and hopefully draw attention to them so they can't finish the job." Insurance analysts and law-enforcement officials concur that the most important factor in an anti-theft system is time: The more time a thief needs to steal a car, the less chance there is it will be stolen.

The range of security devices for cars today is wide, both in price and type. You can spend as little as $5 to $10 for a piece of plastic that makes your expensive cassette player look like an el cheapo A.M. radio, or you can spend upward of $1500 for a remote-controlled system including a siren, ignition and fuel cut-offs, hood locks, window and door controls, and motion and sound sensors.

Alarms and sensors are the most effective systems against vandalism and theft of accessories, say the experts. Protection against theft of the entire car, however, is better left to fuel or starter cut-off switches and hood locks that keep thieves out of the engine compartment.

Many car manufacturers are now building computerized security systems into some of their models. For example, the Chevrolet Corvette has a passive alarm that automatically goes to work when the door is locked. Toyota, Nissan, and Mercedes-Benz make cars with similar systems, and most new BMWs are equipped with a computerized keypad that allows the driver to punch in a code before leaving the car that must be matched upon reentry before the car will start.

The worry of auto theft has never weighed heavy on the minds of California cattle ranchers. And as far as that goes, cattle stealing probably isn't much of a problem either. All the same, in 1985 the California State Assembly passed a bill allowing California cattle ranchers to "brand" their gas-powered stock as well as their hoofed herd.

The bill allows the owner of a registered cattle brand to have his vehicles' license plates inscribed with the same design for a fee of $75 to $85.

Reports are unclear as to why ranchers want their wheels so tagged, but Norm Waters, a Democrat cattle rancher from the town of Plymouth and the chairman of the Assembly Agriculture Committee, called the bill's approval "a big gesture for the cattle industry."

The California Department of Motor Vehicles was against the bill, citing that it would cost $40 to $50 to produce each plate, but the high cost was taken into account by the bill, with excess revenues from the sale of each plate going to agricultural education.

## P. T. Barnum and the Baby Reo

P. T. Barnum couldn't pass up an opportunity to astonish his eager show-goers. In 1906 a car—in any shape or form—drew oohs and ahs from most crowds; but Barnum knew his market and presented the Baby Reo. With production limited to approximately ten, this miniature two-cylinder car was exactly like its full-size sister except that it ran on compressed air. Just how small was it? Well, four midgets could fit into it more easily than a twelve-year-old boy.

# Ford's Vegetable Car

One day back in the early 1930s, Henry Ford strode into his research lab, dumped a greasy bag of chicken bones down on a desk, and said, "See what you can do with these."

This was the first evidence that Ford was serious about building a car out of organic material—and the beginning of an idea that eventually developed into something called the vegetable car.

Ford's researchers later admitted they couldn't make more than a bowl of soup out of the hen-house leftovers, and they didn't have any better luck with the twenty truckloads of cantaloupes Mr. Ford delivered to the lab on another occasion. But Ford was determined to come up with a crop that could be used to make car components, and after extensive tests with thousands of bushels of everything from carrots and cornstalks to cabbages and onions, he finally found magic in the stalk of a soybean plant.

By 1940, Ford researchers had discovered that soybean oil made a superior enamel for automotive paint, and further experiments resulted in a moldable cellulose-fiber plastic that seemed to put Ford's dream, the vegetable car, firmly on the drawing board. Henry Ford's own 1941 Ford sedan had an experimental deck lid made of the new soy plastic, which Ford delighted in pounding with an ax to show skeptics that the lid would withstand blows without a dent or scratch.

In August 1941, the company's first experimental plastic car body appeared on display. But while the famous new car was lightweight and could withstand ten times more shock than steel, its chief engineer later admitted it just wasn't practical. The plastic took too long to cure, and its brittleness made it difficult to mold on a car frame. Also, plastic was more expensive than sheet metal, and the formaldehyde used in its production made the car smell like a mortuary, the chief engineer said.

In spite of the fact that Henry Ford's early vision of a car from the soil never fully became a reality, by 1943 every 1 million V-8 Fords built used 69 million pounds of cotton, 3 million pounds of wool, 350,000 pounds of goat hair, 2 million gallons of molasses, 2 million pounds of linseed, 500,000 bushels of corn—plus acres of soybeans.

In 1943, when a goat actually ate an Illinois license plate made of a soybean-derived fiberboard, old jokes about the vegetable car resurfaced. One would-be sales pitch went, "You don't need to buy a new car every year—just have last year's model warmed over."

## Ten Cars That Didn't Quite Make It

(Limited Production Cars)

| CAR | COMPANY AND LOCATION | YEAR |
|-----|----------------------|------|
| Blackhawk | Stutz Motor Car Co.<br>Indianapolis, Indiana | 1929–30 |

| CAR | COMPANY AND LOCATION | YEAR |
|-----|---------------------|------|
| Brewster | Springfield Manufacturing Co. Springfield, Massachusetts | 1934–36 |
| DeVaux | DeVaux-Hall Motor Corp. Grand Rapids, Michigan | 1931–32 |
| duPont | duPont Motors, Inc. Moore, Pennsylvania | 1930–32 |
| Griffith | Griffith Motors Syosset, White Plains, and Plainview, New York | 1964–66 |
| Henry J. | Kaiser-Frazer Willow Run, Michigan | 1951–54 |
| Imp | International Motor Products Glendale, California | 1949–51 |
| Jordan | Jordan Motor Car Co. Cleveland, Ohio | 1930–31 |
| Mohs | Mohs Seaplane Corp. Madison, Wisconsin | 1967–75 |
| Playboy | Playboy Motor Corp. Buffalo, New York | 1947–51 |

# The Car That Ran on Air and a Secret

Hop in your car, step on the "air," and cruise away smoothly and silently to speeds of 70 miles per hour without ever changing a gear or pushing a clutch.

That was the promise of Los Angeles inventor Frank R. Perry, who in 1945 built a novel auto called the Perrymobile. Although it worked along the same lines as the steamer, using pressure instead of explosive power to turn over the engine, the Perrymobile used a combination of compressed air and a "secret" non-flammable liquid that would vaporize at a much lower temperature than water—about 150 degrees Fahrenheit. The secret liquid was heated by a boiler that could burn anything from butane to crude oil, said Perry, and only one quart of secret liquid was needed, since after use in the cylinder, it went to the radiator and then was returned to the boiler.

The Perrymobile was never tested commercially, but its inventor claimed to have driven it several thousand miles. The entire car weighed only 700 pounds, and the engine, which was mounted on an old Ford chassis, weighed a mere 140 pounds. If run on butane, Perry said, the car would average 60 miles to the gallon.

So, whatever happened to the Perrymobile? That, too, is a secret.

## Armored Cars

The Protective Systems Division of the Tetradyne Corporation in Richardson, Texas, produces made-to-order armored cars, building on production cars from Detroit. The most common automobiles are not Cadillacs and Continentals, which are too conspicuous, but LTDs. Standard requests are for straight-side, Lexan-glass windows; 1¾-inch thick windshields; armor plating that includes protection of the gas tank; and gun racks and gun ports in the front. The cars are said to be impenetrable to .30 caliber rounds.

The year 1922 was the first in which Hudson produced armored cars with quarter-inch-thick armored steel and a safety glass windshield.

One of Franklin D. Roosevelt's more notable cars was the "Sunshine Special," a convertible Lincoln that in 1942 was restyled to provide extra protection for the President. The trip back to the Ford plant resulted in armor plate, bulletproof glass an inch thick, bulletproof tires, space for arms, red warning lights, a siren, and a two-way radio. Final specifications for the automobile: 160-inch wheelbase; 9,300 pounds; V-12 engine; and an additional 6 feet in length.

In 1950, the Truman White House leased ten Lincoln Cosmopolitans with special features such as a 20-inch addition to the wheelbase and 1,600 more pounds; heavy armor; bulletproof glass; disappearing steps on the rear fenders and hand grips for the Secret Service men; two additional folding seats; and head room for the high silk hats that were popular at the time. The President's car also included a vanity case and a writing desk.

President John F. Kennedy's assassination car was an elongated, navy blue, bubble-top Lincoln Continental that included rear-seat illumination, a hand rail to allow the President to stand while riding, interchangeable roofs, flagstaffs on the front fender, and a power-operated back seat that could be raised ten and a half inches from the floor so the President could be seen while staying seated. It was armored much the same as earlier presidential cars.

## Unseen, Unheard—But Not a Secret

In 1909, *Popular Mechanics* magazine reported on a curious new conveyance for members of the U.S. Senate. It seems that a subterranean passage, "somewhat resembling the secret underground exits of medieval castles," had been constructed between the Capitol and a senatorial office a few blocks away and that senators were transported through the tunnel by means of large electric automobiles. Though seemingly surreptitious, the hidden Senate transport system was "not secret," the magazine pointed out, but merely an intelligent use of the most "up-to-date conveyances."

## A Car Custom Made for a City

Few cities have a car as special as New York's 1952 Chrysler parade phaeton. Chrysler only built three of the fancy autos, as a promotional move to show off the best of its new line—the other two went to Detroit and

Los Angeles. Designed to represent the state of the art in luxury, the phaeton featured all-steel construction, pigskin upholstery, and a precision clock in the center of the steering column. It had a back seat big enough for a small crowd, and measuring twenty feet from stem to stern, it was one of the longest cars anywhere.

For three years the phaeton was used to parade distinguished visitors through the streets of the Big Apple, but in 1955, Chrysler took back the phaetons to modernize the bodies. Upon its return to New York, the car continued to be used by the city until 1969. Then it was put into storage and finally due to be junked.

During the 1976 presidential campaign, Jimmy Carter requested a convertible to tour the city, and the phaeton reappeared. After years of storage, it couldn't be readied fast enough for Carter, but the city then decided to restore the old glory wagon. Chrysler chipped in, and soon the phaeton was back on the streets. The governor of Japan was the first bigwig to ride in the newly refurbished car. Then, when the hostages returned from Iran in 1981, the phaeton led their parade through Manhattan.

## Three-Wheelers

Three-wheelers are not uncommon in the car world. The list below represents those innovative marvels that have a place in the annals of auto history.

Airscoot/Aircraft Products Co.
Autoette/Autoette Electric Car Co.
Bassons Star/Bassons Industries
Brogan/B & B Specialty Co.
Californian/Californian Motor Car Co.
Comet/General Developing Co.
Davis/Davis Motor Co.
Diehlmobile/H. L. Diehl Co.
Electra King/B & Z Electric Car Co.
Electrobile/manufacturer unknown
Marketour/Marketour Electric Cars
Morgan/The Morgan Motor Company
Publix/Publix Motor Car Co.
Roadable/Portable Products Corp.
Taylor-Dunn/Taylor-Dunn Manufacturing
Thrif-T/Tri-Wheel Motor Corp.
Tri-Car/manufacturer unknown

## The Amazing Folding Car

You've seen convertible sofas, folding chairs, tables, walls, even folding bikes, but what about a folding car? No?

Well, believe it or not, the Aircraft Products Company of Wichita, Kansas, built one back in the late forties. It was called the Airscoot, and it folded into a package the size of a suitcase, yet it could carry two full-grown men at speeds up to 25 M.P.H. Designed for transporting private plane owners to and from airports, the miniauto weighed only 72 pounds. You just stowed it aboard your aircraft like any other piece of luggage. Once you arrived at your destination, Airscoot took a mere one minute to unfold and assemble, and you were off.

Made primarily of aluminum and magnesium tubing, Airscoot sported a 1-cylinder, 2.6-horsepower engine, and measured 37 inches long and 20 inches tall. It could carry a payload of 450 pounds, carried a gas tank that held 3/10 gallon, and averaged 60 miles to the gallon.

## Presidential Camera Shy

William Howard Taft, the first American President to make regular use of an automobile (a White Steamer), was a persnickity man who, perhaps because of his enormous bulk, was choosy about having his photo taken. Of course, it was difficult to stop photographers from trying to snap the President, but George Robinson, Taft's inventive chauffeur, had a clever way of foiling unwanted shutterbugs while driving the chief executive. Whenever cameramen appeared around Taft's car, Robinson would release a valve on the car that caused huge clouds of steam to engulf the car and its occupants. Before the photographers had a chance to adjust their cameras, Taft would be lost in the dense mist, Robinson would hit the accelerator, and the car would be gone.

# This Diamond Cut Potholes

A smooth ride is something auto manufacturers have always taken great pains to achieve in their products. While most advances along this line have had to do with improvements in wheel suspension, one California inventor took a different approach to the problem of softening the bumps. H. Gordon Hanson of San Lorenzo, California, had the idea that if a car's wheels were configured in a diamond rather than the normal rectangle, it would take road bumps in three places instead of two, thus making the car ride smoother. In 1959, $5000 and 4000 hours after starting the project, Hanson unveiled the Gordon Diamond. The strange-looking auto had one steerable wheel in front, one wheel in back, and two on the sides at the middle for traction and stability. "Driving it on a rough road," said Hanson, "is like cutting diagonally across railroad tracks in a standard car."

When Hanson tried to sell the Diamond idea to a major manufacturer, he aroused the interest of Kaiser-Frazer and Packard, but neither company bought the idea. Did Hanson junk the unusual mobile? No way. He put 95,000 miles on the Diamond before selling it in 1967 to Harrah's Auto Collection in Reno, Nevada.

# Mascots and Hood Ornaments

Mascots and hood ornaments have become hot collectibles—and for a good reason. Many of these small additions are quite beautiful and distinctive. Early mascots were humorous, almost grotesque, but they gave way to the striking graceful ornaments of sleek metal and iced glass. René Lalique is probably the most famous figurehead designer. His glass creations were found on many a man's *grande marque* in the twenties and thirties.

The list below matches some of the more well-known company mascots with their appropriate sponsors.

Auburn—Mercury
Cadillac—Herald, Heron, Goddesses
Chevrolet—Eagle, Viking
Chrysler—Gazelle
Dodge—Ram
Franklin—Lion
Lincoln—Greyhound
Minerva—Helmeted Goddess of Wisdom
Packard—Pelican, Cormorant, Goddess of Speed
Pierce-Arrow—Archer
Pontiac—Indian
Rolls-Royce—Spirit of Ecstasy
Studebaker—Swan
Stutz—Ra (sun god), Sun Dial
Thomas (Flyer)—Eagle on a Globe
Wills-St. Claire—Flying Goose

# If You Can't Make It Fast, Make It Loud

The Model T was never meant to be a race car, but during the 1920s it was just about the *only* car, and if a kid was of a mind to turn something into a hot rod, more often than not it was the innocent-looking Tin Lizzie.

It was possible, with considerable investment, to modify the T into a fairly fast road machine. You could put aluminum pistons in the car, for example, or add a full-pressure oiling system, dual carburetors, a special high-tension magneto, or any number of extras. But if you didn't have the money to make the car faster, you could at least make it louder, which many would-be street racers did.

They did it, most often, by attaching a tin can to the car's tailpipe. The bigger the can, the louder the roar. The bravest of the noise makers went one step farther, says Clark Smith, a mechanic of the day. "Some fellas would put a five-gallon can on the tailpipe and put a handful of shingle nails in it. When the engine revved, the nails would rattle like all getout. You could hear one coming ten miles away."

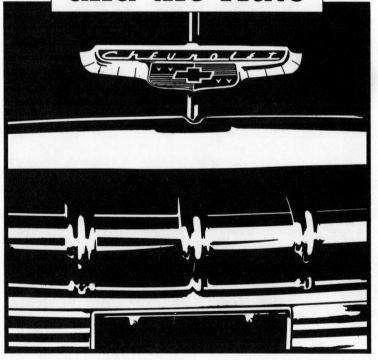

# The Author and the Auto

# she being Brand

she being Brand

-new; and you
know consequently a
little stiff i was
careful of her and(having

thoroughly oiled the universal
joint tested my gas felt of
her radiator made sure her springs were **O.**

**K.**)i went right to it flooded-the-carburetor cranked her

up,slipped the
clutch(and then somehow got into reverse she
kicked what
the hell)next
minute i was back in neutral tried and

again slo-wly;bare,ly nudg.   ing(my

lev-er Right-
oh and her gears being in
A 1 shape passed
from low through
second-in-to-high like
greasedlightning)just as we turned the corner of Divinity

---

avenue i touched the accelerator and give

her the juice,good

                              (it
was the first ride and believe i we was
happy to see how nice she acted right up to
the last minute coming back down by the Public
Gardens i slammed on
the
internalexpanding
&
externalcontracting
brakes Bothatonce and

brought allofher trem**B**
-ling
to a:dead.

stand-
;Still)

e. e. cummings
*is 5*

## Auto Passages

"Why would I want . . . to . . . eat . . . a . . . car?"
Herman said the words very slowly as though he might
be tasting them. "I can tell you. The car is where we are

in America." He paused again and said slowly, "I'm going to eat a car because it's there."

—Harry Crews
Car

The truth is I dislike cars. Whenever I drive a car, I have the feeling I have become invisible. People on the street cannot see you; they only watch your rear fender until it is out of their way.

—Walker Percy
The Moviegoer

Listen to the motor. Listen to the wheels. Listen with your ears and with your hands on the steering wheel; listen with the palm of your hand on the gear-shift lever; listen with your feet on the floor boards. Listen to the pounding old jalopy with all your senses; for a change of tone, a variation of rhythm may mean—a week here? That rattle—that's tappets. Don't hurt a bit. Tappets can rattle till Jesus comes again without no harm. But that thudding as the car moves along—can't hear that—just kind of feel it. Maybe oil isn't gettin' someplace. Maybe a bearing's startin' to go. Jesus, if it's a bearing, what'll we do? Money's goin' fast.

And why's the son-of-a-bitch heat up so hot today? This ain't no climb. Le's look. God Almighty, the fan belt's gone! Here, make a belt outa this little piece a rope. Le's see how long—there. I'll splice the ends. Now take her slow—slow, till we can get to a town. That rope belt won't last long.

'F we can on'y get to California where the oranges grow before this here ol' jug blows up. 'F we on'y can.

And the tires—two layers of fabric worn through. On'y a four-ply tire. Might get a hunderd miles more outa her if we don't hit a rock an' blow her. Which'll we take—a hundred, maybe, miles, or maybe spoil the tube? Which? A hundred miles. Well, that's somepin you got to think about. We got tube patches. Maybe when she goes she'll only spring a leak. How about makin' a boot? Might get five hunderd more miles. Le's go on till she blows.

—John Steinbeck
*The Grapes of Wrath*

The inner-tube Jeeter was attempting to patch again was on the verge of falling into pieces. The tyres themselves were in a condition even more rotten. And the Ford car, fourteen years old that year, appeared as if it would never stand together long enough for Jeeter to put the tyre back on the wheel, much less last until it could be loaded with blackjack for a trip to Augusta. The touring-car's top had been missing for seven or eight years, and the one remaining wing was linked to the body with a piece of rusty baling wire. All the springs and horsehair had disappeared from the upholstery; the children had taken the seats apart to find out what was on the inside, and nobody had made an attempt to put them together again.

The appearance of the automobile had not been improved by the dropping off of the radiator in the road somewhere several years before, and a rusty lard-can with a hole punched in the bottom was wired to the water pipe on top of the engine in its place. The lard-can failed to fill the need for a radiator, but it was much better than nothing. When Jeeter got ready to go somewhere, he filled the lard pail to overflowing, jumped in, and drove until the water splashed out and the engine locked up with heat. He would get out then and look for a creek so he could fill the pail again. The whole car was like that.

—Erskine Caldwell
*Tobacco Road*

When I told Chester I wanted to buy a car, he let me off the hook for his fee, even took me to look at the traps on the car lot. Then I told Chester I didn't want a trap, I wanted a real car.

"That's the way you get a real one," he said. "You make it to suit yourself—Motown just makes them to break down."

We looked at a Pontiac with only 38,000 and a 327. Somebody had lamed in the rear and pushed the trunk into the back seat. There was a clump of hair hanging from the chrome piece around the window. Chester crawled under this car and was gone for almost five minutes, while I was more attracted to a Chevy Impala with a new paint job and a backyard, install-it-yourself convertible top that came down of its own when you pressed a button. Chester came out from under the Pontiac like he had found a snake, then walked over to me grinning.

"She's totaled to hell and back, but the engine's perfect."

—Breece D'J Pancake
"The Salvation of Me"

She was a bad joke, and what Arnie saw in her that day I'll never know. The left side of her windshield was a snarled spiderweb of cracks. The right rear deck was bashed in, and an ugly nest of rust had grown in the paint-scraped valley. The back bumper was askew, the trunk-lid was ajar, and upholstery was bleeding out through several long tears in the seat covers, both front and back. It looked as if someone had worked on the upholstery with a knife. One tire was flat. The others were bald enough to show the canvas cording. Worst of all, there was a dark puddle of oil under the engine block.

Arnie had fallen in love with a 1958 Plymouth Fury, one of the long ones with the big fins.

—Stephen King
*Christine*


The Ford Garage and the Buick Garage, competent one-story brick and cement buildings opposite each other. Old and new cars on grease-blackened concrete floors. Tire advertisements. The roaring of a tested motor; a racket which beat at the nerves. Surly young men in khaki union-overalls. The most energetic and vital places in town.

—Sinclair Lewis
*Main Street*


Prohibition had not had much effect on such places. . . . The Farmers Hotel in Turnersville was beginning to enjoy a certain limited popularity among our crowd. It was an out-of-the-way place and cheap, and the old jokes about Turnersville became passé, in a few years the name of the village became synonymous with drinking. "Turnersville? Nine o'clock?" we would say, and it was all we needed to say. Almost any night you would see family cars parked outside: Joe Choate's Wills Ste. Claire,

Charley Lloyd's Packard roadster, Mary Stauffer's Oakland coupe, Whit Hofman's Mercer phaeton, Stuffy Reifsnyder's Daniels, as well as the Dodges and Buicks of the boys using the family car.

—John O'Hara
"A Few Trips and Some Poetry"

An automobile was coming up the hill from North Avenue. As it drew closer he saw it was a black 45-horsepower Pope-Toledo Runabout. . . . The car came past his house, made a loud noise and swerved into the telephone pole. . . . The driver and the passenger were standing in the street looking at the car: it had big wheels with pneumatic tires and wooden spokes painted in black enamel. It had brass headlamps in front of the radiator and brass sidelamps over the fenders. It had tufted upholstery and double side entrances. It did not appear to be damaged.

—E. L. Doctorow
*Ragtime*

He saw me looking with admiration at his car.
"It's pretty isn't it, old sport!" He jumped off to give me a better view. "Haven't you ever seen it before?"
I'd seen it. Everybody had seen it. It was a rich cream color, bright with nickel, swollen here and there in its monstrous length with triumphant hat-boxes and supperboxes and tool-boxes, and terraced with a labyrinth of windshields that mirrored a dozen suns.

—F. Scott Fitzgerald
*The Great Gatsby*

Dad had bought the automobile a year before we moved. It was our first car, and cars still were a novelty. Of course, that had been a surprise, too. He had taken us all for a walk and had ended up at a garage where the car had been parked.

Although Dad made his living by redesigning complicated machinery, so as to reduce the number of human motions required to operate it, he never really understood the mechanical intricacies of our automobile. It was a gray Pierce Arrow, equipped with two bulb horns and an electric Klaxon, which Dad would try to blow all at the same time when he wanted to pass anyone. The engine hood was long and square, and you had to raise it to prime the petcocks on cold mornings.

Dad had seen the car in the factory and fallen in love with it. The affection was entirely one-sided and unrequited. He named it Foolish Carriage because, he said, it was foolish for any man with as many children as he to think he could afford a horseless carriage.

The contraption kicked him when he cranked, spat oil in his face when he looked into its bowels, squealed when he mashed the brakes, and rumbled ominously when he shifted gears. Sometimes Dad would spit, squeal, and rumble back. But he never won a single decision.

—Frank B. Gilbreth, Jr. and Ernestine Gilbreth Carey
*Cheaper by the Dozen*


When we returned from England, we bought a car. We had ordered it through my parents from folders they had sent us, and, though its shade of blue was more naive, more like a robin's egg, than we had expected, this '55 Ford proved an excellent buy. Whether being shuffled from side to side of West Eighty-fifth Street every morning or being rammed in second gear up a washed-out mountain road in Vermont, it never complained. In New York, hot tar from a roof-patching job rained onto its innocent paint, and in Vermont its muffler was racked and rent on a shelf of rock, and in Massachusetts it wallowed, its hot clutch stinking, up from repeated graves of snow. Not only sand and candy wrappers accumulate in a car's interior, but heroisms and instants of communion. We in America make love in our cars, and listen to ball games, and plot our wooing of the dollar: small wonder the landscape is sacrificed to these dreaming vehicles of our ideal and onrushing manhood.

—John Updike
"Packed Dirt, Churchgoing, A Dying Cat, A Traded Car"

"Just recently he bought this new car," Zelda went on, "with the rest of that money. It has a tape deck and all the furnishings. Eli doesn't like it, or so I heard. That car reminds him of his girl. . . . So the insurance explained the car. More than that it explained why everyone treated the car with special care. Because it was new, I had thought. Still, I had noticed all along that nobody seemed proud of it except for King and Lynette. Nobody leaned against the shiny blue fenders, rested elbows on the hood, or set paper plates there while they ate. Aurelia didn't even want to hear King's tapes. It was as if the car was wired up to something. As if it might give off a shock when touched. Later, when Gordie came, he brushed the glazed chrome and gently tapped the tires with his toes. He would not go riding in it, either, even though King urged his father to experience how smooth it ran. We heard the car move off, wheels crackling in the gravel and cinders. Then it was quiet for a long time again.

—Louise Erdrich
*Love Medicine*

My grandfather didn't want an automobile at all; he was forced to buy one. A banker, president of the older Bank of Jefferson, the first bank in Yoknapatawpha County, he believed then and right on to his death many years afterward, by which time everybody else even in Yoknapatawpha County had realised that the automobile had come to stay, that the motor vehicle was an insolvent phenomenon like last night's toadstool and, like the fungus, would vanish with tomorrow's sun. But Colonel Sartoris, president of the newer, the mushroom Merchants and Farmers Bank, forced him to buy one. Or rather, another insolvent, a dreamy myopic gentian–eyed mechanical wizard named Buffaloe, compelled him to. Because my grandfather's car wasn't even the first one in Jefferson. (I dont count Manfred de Spain's red E.M.F. racer. Although De Spain owned it and drove it daily through Jefferson streets for several years, it had no more place in the decorous uxorious pattern of a community than Manfred himself did, both of them being incorrigible and bachelor, not in the town but on it and up to no good like one prolonged unbroken Saturday night even while Manfred was actually mayor, its very scarlet color being not even a scornful defiance of the town but rather a kind of almost inattentive disavowal.)

So he bought the automobile, and Boon found his soul's lily maid, the virgin's love of his rough and innocent heart. It was a Winton Flyer. (This was the first one he—we—owned, before the White Steamer which Grandfather traded it for when Grandmother finally decided two years later that she couldn't bear the smell of gasoline at all.) You cranked it by hand while standing in front of it, with no more risk (provided you had remembered to take it out of gear) than a bone or two in your forearm; it had kerosene lamps for night driving and when rain threatened five or six people could readily put up the top and curtains in ten or fifteen minutes, and Grandfather himself equipped it with a kerosene lantern, a new axe and a small coil of barbed wire attached to a light block and tackle for driving beyond the town limits. With which equipment it could—and did once, of which I shall speak presently—go as far as Memphis. Also, all of us, grandparents, parents, aunts, cousins and children, had special costumes for riding in it, consisting of veils, caps, goggles, gauntlet gloves and long shapeless throat-close neutral-colored garments called dusters, of which I shall also speak later.

—William Faulkner
*The Reivers*

He also kept some broken-down cars around that he liked to tinker on. In the first stages of their affair my wife had told me he "collected antique cars." Those were her words. I'd seen some of his cars parked in front of his house when I'd driven by there trying to see what I could see. Old 1950s and 1960s, dented cars with torn seat covers. They were junkers, that's all. I knew. I had his number. We had things in common, more than just driving old cars and trying to hold on for dear life to the same woman.

—Raymond Carver
"Where Is Everyone?"

THE AUTHOR AND THE AUTO

It was in a handsome two-seater Buick, canary-yellow, with rakish wire-spoked wheels, that Garth and Little Goldie eloped, and in a smart little fire-engine-red Fiat with a cream-colored convertible top and polished hubcaps . . . that Christabel and Demuth Hodge eloped one fine autumn morning, driving, for brief periods during their gay, reckless, euphoric flight, at speeds of a hundred miles per hour despite the winding mountain roads. It was a super-charged Auburn, chalk-white, with gray upholstery and exposed exhaust pipes, of gleaming chromium, another sporty two-seater, that carried away, into the labyrinthian shadows of an unnamed foreign city, possibly Rome, the beautiful young actress "Yvette Bonner." . . .

—Joyce Carol Oates
*Bellefleur*

"We're just beginning now," said Number One. "Automobile design is a very complicated art. An art. That's exactly what it is. Modern, functional art. A primary collage of our technocratic society. That's what it is, gentlemen. The Model T of Henry Ford does not belong in the Smithsonian. A more proper place for it would be in the Metropolitan Museum of Art."

—Harold Robbins
*The Betsy*

"Someone mentioned breakthroughs," Adam answered. "The most important ones, which we can see coming, are in materials which will let us design a whole new breed of vehicles by the mid- or late '70s. Take metals. Instead of solid steel which we're using now, honeycomb steel is coming; it'll be strong, rigid, yet incredibly lighter—meaning fuel economy; also it'll absorb an impact better than conventional steel—a safety plus. Then there are new metal alloys for engines and components. We anticipate one which will allow temperature changes from a hundred degrees to more than two thousand degrees Fahrenheit, in seconds, with minor expansion only. Using that, we can incinerate the remainder of unburned fuel causing air pollution. Another metal being worked on is one with a retention technique to 'remember' its original shape. If you crumple a fender or a door, you'll apply heat or pressure and the metal will spring back the way it was before. Another alloy we expect will allow cheap production of reliable, high-quality wheels for gas turbine engines."

Elroy Braithwaite added, "That last is one to watch. If the internal combustion engine goes eventually, the gas turbine's most likely to move in. There are plenty of problems with a turbine for cars—it's efficient only at high power output, and you need a costly heat exchanger if you aim not to burn pedestrians. But they're *solvable* problems, and being worked on."

"Okay," *The Wall Street Journal* said. "So that's metals. What else is new?"

"Something significant, and coming soon for every car, is an on-board computer." Adam glanced at A. P. "It will be small, about the size of a glove compartment."

"A computer to do what?"

"Just about anything; you name it. It will monitor engine components—plugs, fuel injection, all the others. It will control emissions and warn if the engine is polluting. And in other ways it will be revolutionary."

"Name some," *Newsweek* said.

"Part of the time the computer will think for drivers and correct mistakes, often before they realize they're made. One thing it will mastermind is sensory braking—

brakes applied individually on every wheel so a driver can never lose control by skidding. A radar auxiliary will warn if a car ahead is slowing or you're following too close. In an emergency the computer could decelerate and apply brakes automatically, and because a computer's reactions are faster than humans there should be a lot less rear-end collisions. There'll be the means to lock on to automatic radar control lanes on freeways, which are on the way, with space satellite control of traffic flow not far behind."

—Arthur Hailey
*Wheels*

*Bud:* "I see kids ambling up and down Lake in their little transbucket Mustangs, it's totally ridiculous to me. I am unable to understand this. I remember when a guy'd work his butt off to make something worth being seen in—chopped, channeled, bored, and stroked. Dual quads, scavenger pipes, Baby Moons, big Offy manifold, flames painted on the hood, dingleberries in the window, carpet on the floor, fur around the mirror—I mean, we did a *number* on it. There was pride at one time. Now, as I say, it's ludicrous. These guys have nothing and they don't even know it. They don't care."

*Art:* "There was something under the hood in those days—you knew, because you'd *put* it there—and if you didn't have it, you kept off the street or got blown out of the water in a hurry. I had a full-house Ford—four on the floor, geared down deep. When you stuck your foot in it, she'd lay rubber into next week. Other day, I'm coming home from work in my wife's car—my *wife's* car, this *sled*—and a kid pulls up at the stoplight in a *Rambler* and guns it. One of the most pitiful sounds I ever

heard. I am ready to weep. Light turns green, I ooze
away in the slushbox, and this kid can't locate first gear.
It makes you sick to see it."

—Garrison Keillor
"Plainfolks: A Handbook of Survival
Skills, Folkways, Practical Wisdom, and Useful Information,
Compiled from Original Sources
and Reflecting 'The Way It Used
to Be' "

# Ten Early Accounts of Transcontinental Trips

1. *A Family Tour from Ocean to Ocean: Being an account of the first amateur motor car journey from
the Pacific to the Atlantic, whereby J. M. Murdock
and family, in their 1908 Packard "Thirty" touring car,
incidentally broke the transcontinental record*
Jacob M. Murdock
Detroit, Michigan: Packard Motor Car Co., 1908
2. *Coast to Coast in a Brush Runabout 1908*
Florence M. Trinkle
Los Angeles, California: Floyd Clymer Publications,
1952
Seventeenth transcontinental auto trip
3. *Veil, Duster and Tire Iron*
Alice Huyler Ramsey

Covina, California: Castle Press, 1961
First trip by a woman driver
4. *5000 Miles Overland. Wonderful Performance of a Wonderful Car. The Story of Miss Scott's Journey Overland*
Overland Automobile Company
Toledo, Ohio: Overland Automobile Company, 1910
First solo trip by a woman driver
5. *Overland by Auto in 1913. Diary of a Family Tour from California to Indiana*
Estelle McNutt Copeland
Indianapolis, Indiana: Indiana Historical Society, 1981
6. *Across the Continent by the Lincoln Highway*
Effie Price Gladding
New York: Brentano's, 1915
7. *By Motor to the Golden Gate*
Emily Post
New York and London: D. Appleton and Company, 1916
8. *From San Diego, California to Washington, D.C. Being a Descriptive Account of the First Official Trip by Automobile over Southern National Highway*
William Benjamin Gross
San Diego, 1916
9. *Roaming American Highways*
John Thomson Faris
New York: Farrar & Rinehart, Inc., Publishers, 1931
10. *Sweet Land*
Lewis Stiles Gannett
New York: Doubleday, Doran & Company, Inc., 1934
Essays and anecdotes on an 8,631-mile journey

## Five Well-Told Cross-Country Adventures

1. *Air Conditioned Nightmare*   Henry Miller
2. *Around About America*   Erskine Caldwell
3. *Free Air*   Sinclair Lewis
4. *Short Drive, Sweet Chariot*   William Saroyan
5. *Travels with Charlie*   John Steinbeck

## Ten Novels About Cars

1. *Car*   Harry Crews
2. *Wheels*   Arthur Hailey
3. *The Last Convertible*   Anton Myrer
4. *The Betsy*   Harold Robbins
5. *Christine*   Stephen King
6. *Hot Rod*   Henry Gregro Felsen
7. *David White and the Electric Wonder Car*   W. E. Butterworth
8. *Tom Swift and His Electric Runabout or the Speediest Car on the Road*   Victor Appleton, Jr.
9. *Grand National Racer*   Margaret Ogan
10. *The Car Thief*   Theodore Weesner

# The Ballade of the Automobile

When our yacht sails seaward on steady keel
    And the wind is moist with the breath of brine
And our laughter tells of our perfect weal,
    We may carol the praises of ruby wine;
But if, automobiling, my woes combine
    And fuel gives out in my road-machine
And it's sixteen miles to that home of mine—
    Then ho! for a gallon of gasoline!

When our coach rides smoothly on iron-shod wheel
    With a deft touch guiding each taut drawn line
And the inn ahead holds a royal meal,
    We may carol the praises of ruby wine;
But when, on some long and steep incline,
    In a manner entirely unforeseen
The motor stops with a last sad whine—
    Then ho! for a gallon of gasoline!

When the air is crisp and the brooks congeal
    And our sleigh glides on with a speed divine
While the gay bells echo with peal on peal,
    We may carol the praises of ruby wine;
But when, with perverseness most condign,
    In the same harsh snowstorm, cold and keen,
My auto stops at the six-mile sign—
    Then ho! for a gallon of gasoline!

---

When Yacht or Coach Club fellows dine
We may carol the praises of ruby wine;
But when Automobile Clubmen convene
Then ho! for a gallon of gasoline!

—Ellis Parker Butler

# Twenty-five Short Stories for the Car Buff

"Tin Lizzie" J. Dos Passos
"First Auto" L. Lenski
"Brave Automobiles" A. Robles
"Benny and the Birddogs" M. K. Rawlings
"The Motor Car" A. Clarke
"A Vintage Thunderbird" A. Beattie
"Cadillac Flambé" R. Ellison
"Selling Miss Minerva" E. D. Biggers
"Arminta and the Automobile" C. B. Loomis
"You Can Wreck It" W. Elder
"Elephant's Board and Keep" E. H. Porter
"Chariot of Fire" E.S.P. Ward
"The Phantom Mercury of Nevada" D. Kranes
"Joanna Godden's Joy Ride" S. Kaye–Smith
"Tinkle and Family Take a Ride" K. Kelm
"Call of the Carburetor" S. B. Leacock
"The Legend of Joe Lee" J. D. MacDonald
"The Cost of the Car" D. L. Peters
"Encounter in Illinois" R. M. Coates

"The Seven Passenger Nash"  R. Burmester
"The Locking Gas-Cap"  M. Liben
"Old Enough to Drive"  S. McNeil
"The Cat"  D. Woolf
"A Plague of Cars"  L. Tushnet
"Moxon's Master"  A. Bierce

# Twenty-five More Short Stories for the Car Buff

"1924 Cadillac for Sale"  W. Saroyan
"Auto-da-fé"  R. Zelazney
"Car Sinister"  G. Wolfe
"Internal Combustion"  L. S. De Camp
"The Floating Truth"  G. Paley
"Sedan DeVille"  B. N. Malzberg
"California Plates"  J. Annie Crace
"From One Generation to Another"  A. Bennett
"While the Auto Waits"  O. Henry
"The Automobile That Wouldn't Run"  E. Caldwell
"New Model"  H. Titus
"Inside and Out"  H. K. Webster
"Sally"  I. Asimov
"Eldorado"  L. Furman
"Romance in a Twenty-first-Century Used Car Lot"
R. F. Young
"The Big Beast"  P. D. Boles
"Red Camaro"  J. R. Kornblatt
"4: Lincoln Sedan Deadline"  J. Gores

"The Ultimate Automobile"  G. MacQuarrie
"Still Trajectories"  B. W. Aldiss
"The Motormaniacs"  L. Osbourne
"Adjustment"  O. R. Cohen
"Thing of Beauty"  D. Knight
"The Perfect Crime"  E. Schwartz
"A Thing About Cars!"  B. Lumley

# Twenty-five Memorable Racing Movies

*The Big Wheel*  1950
*Bobby Deerfield*  1977
*Bullitt*  1968
*The Crowd Roars*  1932
*Death Race 2000*  1976
*The Drivin' Fool*  1923
*Grand Prix*  1966
*The Great Race*  1965
*The Green Helmet*  1961
*Gumball Rally*  1976
*Heart Like a Wheel*  1983
*Johnny Dark*  1954
*The Last American Hero*  1973
*Le Mans*  1971
*The Love Bug*  1969
*To Please a Lady*  1950
*The Racers*  1955
*Roaring Road*  1926

*Six-Cylinder Love*   1923
*Speedway*   1968
*Spinout*   1966
*Thunder Alley*   1967
*Thunder in Carolina*   1967
*Thunder Road*   1958
*Winning*   1969

# Ten Recorded Comedy Routines and Satires

1. "Continental Steel"   Robert Klein/*New Teeth*
2. "The Driving Lesson"   Bob Newhart/*The Best of Bob Newhart*
3. "Duke of Madness Motors"   Firesign Theatre/*Dear Friends*
4. "Fat Boy"   Lenny Bruce/*Thank You Masked Man*
5. "Prairie Home Companion"   Garrison Keillor
   (There is a wealth of auto lore in radio legend Keillor's stories of Lake Wobegon.)
6. "Profiles in Courage"   National Lampoon/*Radio Dinner*
7. "Sing a Song of Sports Cars"   Riverside Records
8. "Sports Car Songs"   Electra Records
9. "Toad Away"   Firesign Theatre/*Forward into the Past*
10. "200 M.P.H."   Bill Cosby/*TT*

# Cars of the
# Future

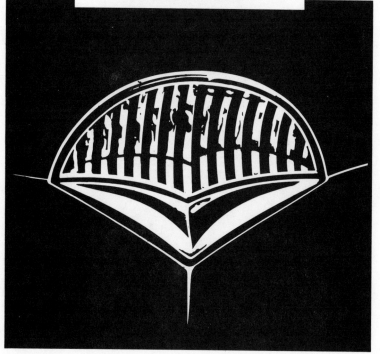

# Engines

When visitors to the first-ever National Automobile Show in New York City were asked which motor they preferred in a car, there was no contest: Electric was the overwhelming choice. Second place went to steam engines. And lagging a distant third with less than 5 percent of the vote was the gasoline engine, which many thought would never last.

"Noxious, noisy, unreliable and elephantine, it vibrates so violently as to loosen one's dentures. The automobile industry will surely burgeon in America, but this motor will not be a factor," one critic wrote.

In addition to a general dissatisfaction with the obstreperousness of these gas-gobbling monsters, there was widespread fear at the show that gas-powered engines could actually explode, spraying showgoers with shrapnel. After all, they ran on just about anything flammable, including stove gas, lamp oil, naphtha, kerosene, benzine, mineral spirits, alcohol, as well as the fairly new fuel called gasoline. *Motor World*, one of the early automotive publications, even referred to gas-powered cars as "explosives." And the public's nerves were nothing quelled by the fact that show officials summoned a standby bucket brigade each time an "explosive" was cranked.

That first show was held in November 1900. Just three

years later, at the 1903 auto show, the number of cars with four-stroke internal combustion gasoline engines had gone up sharply. The quick change was a big surprise to casual followers of the automobile movement, but auto engineers had seen it coming. Steamers were too slow in getting up power, and by 1910 steam-powered cars were on the way out. (The Stanley Steamer continued production into the late 1920s, and one or two other steamer makes struggled into the thirties.) Electric cars held out until about 1915, but they too gave way to the once-hopeless gas machine.

From its inception (Etienne Lenoir of France put together the first four-wheeled gas-powered vehicle in 1860), the gasoline engine has taken any number of forms. Before 1900 it was usually a single-cylinder, two-stroke job, though the variety of configurations developed with this simple powerplant is mind boggling. Soon, bigger gas engines became more prominent. When *Cosmopolitan* magazine published a complete guide to "Gasoline Motor Cars" in 1906, 13 models had 1-cylinder engines, 54 had 2-cylinders, 5 came with 3-cylinder engines, and 59 autos were equipped with 4 cylinders. There was also one 6-cylinder car, built in Detroit by a company called Ford, which sold for $2,500, and one car with a V-8 engine made in Redondo Beach, California. It was called the Coyote. Neither of these last two models survived very long.

Packard was the first to make a 12-cylinder car, in 1916, but cylinder numbers went their highest in the 1930s, when Cadillac, Marmon, and Packard all came out with V-16s. It wasn't long, however, before auto manufacturers realized these huge engines just weren't practical. For the next forty years 6- and 8-cylinder cars were the norm. But during the 1970s the 4-cylinder engine made an overwhelming comeback, and now it seems possible, say the experts, that 2-cylinder cars could also return.

Who knows? One-cylinder cars could come around again. Probably at the turn of the century.

## An Enlightening Idea

Attempts to foresee the future of the car industry have often produced little more than future laughs, but occasionally seemingly screwy ideas become reality. For example, in 1948 a man wrote in to *Popular Science* magazine's "I'd Like To See Them Make . . . " column with his wish: He wanted to see cars with a wireless dashboard cigarette lighter—a gadget with a hot element at the end of a cone, say—so the driver could keep his eyes on the road when using it. Perhaps he also wrote a letter to a manufacturer, since shortly afterward, the lighter he describes became standard equipment on just about every kind of car, and remains so today.

## Crystal Ball

In 1975, *Motor Trend* magazine asked a number of automobile experts to look into the crystal ball and predict the future: what would the automobile industry be like in the year 2000? Below is a sampling of their replies, with their titles at the time of the interview.

The automobile will be obsolete for urban transportation by the year 2000, but will be used for non-city travel. I look for electric cars . . . electric mass transit . . . possibly a new vehicle propulsion system.

—Paul J. Brown
Director, Safety Research Laboratory
National Highway Traffic Safety Administration
U.S. Dept. of Transportation

A wise man once said that the best predictor of future human behavior is how people behaved in the past. Automobiles are designed and built by human beings, so I expect we will make as much progress in the next 25 years as we did in the past 25.

—Gerald C. Myers
Group Vice-President—Product
American Motors Corporation

Aerodynamic torture of innocent air must cease. A 60 mpg, two-passenger commuter car is not only possible but an academic must for our energy survival. Without mobility there can be no prosperity. Period!

—Alex Sarantos Tremulis
Independent Designer

The future of the automobile rests on a simple basic fact—people love cars and will work hard and make sacrifices in order to satisfy their desire. The type of engine will certainly change (my personal bet is electric), but individuals will continue to demand a personal vehicle that will take them from where they want to go.

—Arjay Miller
Dean, Stanford University
Graduate School of Business

The automobile industry is a growth industry and it will always be one. It has to be, because personal transportation isn't going away and over the long run there must be a growing number of vehicles to carry a growing population and its goods from one place to another. I can't tell you precisely what automobiles will be like in the year 2000, but I can give you this much of a prediction: they will still move on four wheels and be powered by combustion engines fueled by liquid petroleum.

—Lee A. Iacocca
President
Ford Motor Company

(Early the next year, Iacocca was quoted as saying: "Three years ago, how did I know that the name of the game would be mpgs instead of how fast you can go from a stoplight.")

# That's Nothin' New

Enough generations have passed since the early innovations of the auto industry that memory serves little purpose, old ideas have been reconstituted and have reappeared in fresh packaging as "new." A new way to sell a car, maybe, but quite often, nothing really new.

Do you remember, for example, how bucket seats became all the rage during the sixties? Impressed by a barrage of snappy advertising, one felt certain bucket seats were at least a relatively new invention, but Henry Ford's first Model A had bucket seats, around 1905.

Or what about ads of a few years back touting the

powerful virtues of new cars with "overhead cams" and "overhead valves"? New? Nope. Those same features were originally introduced on a car made by the Wilkinson Motor Car Co. in 1898.

Was the Volkswagen Beetle the first car with a rear engine and horizontally opposed pistons? Hardly. America's 1905 Knox had an engine with opposed pistons, and an auto known as the Hertel carried its engine in back in 1896.

In the 1980s, to have a really modern car you must have one with front-wheel drive, right? True, but in 1900 the Pennington Car Co. made a front-wheel-drive (FWD) car, and it wasn't even the first. Steamers and electrics had used FWD for years.

When Felix Wankel built a rotary gas engine in 1955, how many would have said it wasn't the first? How many would have known that Elwood Haynes made one in 1893?

And the list goes on. So the next time you hear of some new auto innovation, remember it ain't necessarily new.

## Next Stop, Topeka!

Enter your trip destination coordinates into the control panel; sit back and listen to the voice of a charming man or woman tell you your ETA (estimated time of arrival), give you the latest on your stocks, or describe the choice of hotels at your next stop; then just recline with a good book or conduct business over the phone at your side.

Various satellites are safely navigating your vehicle to its destination.

No, you are not riding in the spaceship Enterprise; you are simply "driving" a standard automobile of the near future, according to researchers at just about every major car manufacturer in the U.S. and Japan in 1984.

By 1986, auto research engineers expect automatic satellite navigation for cars to be reality. Satellites will tell the car when and where to turn, stop, and accelerate, and the car will track itself on its own video screen, they say. Of course, humans will still have to tell the computerized cars where to go, and if you push a wrong button, who knows?—you might end up doing some sightseeing you never planned on.

## The New Armored Car

Blast it with a machine gun, bomb it, or blow out its tires with an M-16—this car would drive away as if nothing ever happened.

This was the new armored car of the 1970s, which several custom car companies began to build in response to a new demand for a safer, more secure car for the VIPs of the world. If you felt threatened enough, and had the dough—up to $245,000, excluding the cost of the car—you could get your standard Cadillac limousine equipped with enough protective equipment to stop an army of terrorists or thwart the most conniving kidnapper.

One company offered customers custom-made armored cars with two levels of protection. The basic model was designed to protect passengers from revolvers, submachine guns, and ordinary hand grenades. The deluxe version was said to resist small land mines, large grenades, Molotov cocktails, and small explosive devices.

The first step in making one of these cars attack-proof was to insert heavy gauge steel sheathing between the body shell and the car's inner panels, as well as behind the front and back seats, under the floorboards and in the roof. This could add from 500 to 1300 pounds to the car. Next, they would install an explosion-proof fuel tank, bullet-proof glass, reinforced bumpers for ramming, and tire safety rollers that would keep the car moving at top speed after the tires had been blown out. Also, various modifications would be carried out to make the car as fireproof as possible.

Then there was the big-time armored car—the traveling fortress, the civilian tank that could not only withstand terrorist attacks, but could fight back in a variety of interesting and lethal ways.

One such car was built for the Shah of Iran in 1979. It looked like a standard '79 Caddy, but came equipped with front and rear machine-gun ports; an emission system that could spill oil on the road or spray tear gas or sleeping gas up to 50 feet; a hidden transmitter, so the car could be tracked anywhere; a hand-held bomb sniffer; an electronic watchdog that told if the auto had been tampered with; a remote control ignition device that would start the car a quarter-mile away; and infrared glasses for the driver, to be worn for getaways in fog, smoke, or total darkness. Unwanted poassengers of this car were in extreme danger. Under the seat of the passenger side were three shotgun shells, pointed up. One wrong move and the unwanted could get his tail blown off. And as a last-ditch measure, hidden in the trunk was a high-powered minibike that could cruise at speeds of 65 M.P.H.

One of these armored cars proved its worth in 1979, when four oil company executives were attacked by terrorists during a South American revolution. After forcing the car to a halt with a herd of animals, the terrorists opened fire on the car. When they realized their bullets weren't penetrating, they tried to hack it open with axes. At this point, one of the executives unloaded his pistol through one of the car's gunports while another pushed a button that unleashed a cloud of tear gas on the assailants. The driver then hit the gas and made the getaway.

## The Sun Makes It Run

First there was the steam car. Then came the electric. The gas-powered buggy was next. Now, the solar age is beginning to have an impact on the automobile. In the summer of 1984, an experimental car called the TSAR Phoenix (Trans-America Solar Auto Run) made the first successful solar-powered cross-country trip—2300 miles, from San Diego to Jacksonville, Florida. Put together by a team of engineers, technicians, and teachers from Missouri, the three-wheeled Phoenix used 16 photovoltaic panels to power a small electric motor. The panels, which lay like a large flat trailer behind the car's low-slung skeletal front section, generated up to 640 watts, which sent the sun wagon along at average speeds of

15 to 20 M.P.H. For the summer of 1985, the car's inventors planned an attempt to break the world solar-powered speed record of 24 M.P.H. This sounds strangely like the automobile's pioneer days. Got any stock in the oil companies?

## Power of the Printed Word

In 1984, two professors at the Florida Institute of Technology successfully tested a new auto fuel whose primary ingredient is shredded newspaper. Running on a mixture of ordinary gasoline and the new "news" fuel, the test car reportedly achieved 34 miles per gallon, compared to 27 mpg on gas alone. Additional advantages of the newsprint-based fuel extender include that it's inexpensive to make and it doesn't tax food supplies as some biomass-derived fuel alcohols could potentially do.

## A Breather for Marathoners

When the Summer Olympic Committee planned the marathon running events in Los Angeles in 1984, they banned all cars from the courses. L. A.'s smog was bad enough without a camera car's exhaust wafting into the runners' faces. But since the show must go on, ABC-TV had a smogless electric van developed that is said to have since revolutionized sports coverage. Called the Uniq Turbo Electrek, the futuristic-looking vehicle ran on a 43-hp battery-powered electric motor with a small Chrysler turbo engine as backup. Carrying a 300-pound capacity load of camera equipment, the mobile unit quietly kept pace with lead marathoners, allowing the TV audience to hear every footstep and labored breath.

# The Car of the Eighties

Early predictions as to the future of the automobile have produced some amusing images and ideas. Take, for example, the vision of Plymouth chief engineer Jack Charipar, when in 1959 he was asked by *Popular Science* magazine to describe the car of the 1980s:

● First, said Charipar, because superhighways and automatic driving controls will make very high speeds possible, automobiles will have to be extremely streamlined, with large tailfins for stability. Windows will be fixed and molded into the streamlined shape, perhaps even enclosing the entire top of the car with "transparent steel."

● There will be only two basic auto types: sedan and station wagon, but a variety of new options will allow the buyer to order anything from a simple two-door utility car to a "magnificent suburban land yacht."

● Car bodies will be lower—as low as 51 inches, which

is the limit unless occupants lie prone—but width and length shouldn't change much. The main body of the car—hood, engine, passenger compartment, trunk—will sit below the wheels, and the fenders will be close-fitting "blisters" that stick up, like fenders on salt flats speed-record machines. Thus, cars will have only 4 or 5 inches' road clearance, and utility vehicles will need adjustable suspensions for adequate clearance on rougher roads.

• Cars will be made of "wraparound sheet metal" requiring no paint or finish, said Charipar. Instead, the metal will have color fused into it.

• Gas tanks will be obsolete. Instead, fuel will be stored in a system of small plastic containers tucked into odd nooks and crannies.

• Brakes will be mounted away from the wheels for more efficient cooling. But they'll need help on high speed stops from "aerodynamic flaps that open out of the fender fins."

One thing that won't change, Charipar concluded, is the need for change. Manufacturers will still have to redesign cars every year or so in order to meet the demand for new styling.

Well, he got that right, anyway.

## Fastest Car of the Future

Ever since Frenchman Chasseloup-Laubat went 24.3 M.P.H. in 1898 to set what is widely regarded as the first world automobile speed record, bettering the mark has been the supreme goal of all motor-sports. At this writing, the official record stands at 633.468 M.P.H., set by Richard Noble in 1983. But it was thirteen years between this record and the previous mark of 622.407 M.P.H., set by Gary Gabelich in 1970, and the difference ain't that great— a mere 11 M.P.H. So is there a land speed limit for all time, future included? If so, Craig Breedlove doesn't want to hear about it.

A five-time world speed record holder himself—his last being 600.6 M.P.H. in 1965—Breedlove has a new car and a new goal for the future. His car (it looks more like the starship Enterprise) is called the Spirit of America Sonic II, and his goal is Mach 1, the sound barrier—741 M.P.H. He'll attempt the goal sometime in the spring of 1986, either at Edwards Air Force Base in California's Mojave Desert or Blackrock Desert in Gerlach, Nevada. If he reaches the mark, Breedlove will break Noble's record by 108 M.P.H., but even that won't satisfy him. Evidently, Breedlove's ultimate plans with the 40-ft., $1.1-million Sonic II include a shot at the 1000 M.P.H. mark. How fast is 1000 M.P.H.? A mile every 3.6 seconds.

# In the Year 2000 . . .

For a long time, people have used the year 2000 as a symbol of the foreseeable future. Now that time is not far away, and it's much easier to predict the changes that should take place by then. Where will the automobile fit in at the turn of the century? According to the Omni Future Almanac of 1982, more or less as follows:

Due to the effects of inflation, the average price of an American compact car will have risen from $5,200 in 1980 to $30,000 in 2000. A gallon of gas will go to $4 by 1990, but back down to $2 by 2000.

Whereas the average American family income will go from its 1980 level of $15,500 per year to $24,600 per year, the percentage of income spent on transportation will actually go down—from 15.6% in 1980, to 12.6% in 2000.

Compucars—highly computerized automobiles—will achieve new levels of efficiency: Computer-assisted fuel flow and engine control will enable cars to average 100 mpg under normal driving conditions.

Computer-controlled cars will also greatly reduce traffic congestion in urban areas and decrease air pollution from 70 million tons a year to 27 million tons.

There will be a 50 percent increase in the number of cars on American roads between 1980 and 2000.

Just short of one half of the planet's estimated oil supply of 2,000 billion barrels will be gone, approximately half of that amount having been used in the last twenty-five years of the twentieth century.

From *Omni Future Almanac,* copyright 1982 by Omni Publications International, Ltd. Published by Harmony Books, One Park Avenue, New York, NY 10016.

# You and the World of Cars

# Automobile Archives and Reference Collections

American Motors Historical File
14250 Plymouth Road
Detroit, MI 48232

Antique Automobile Club of America
501 West Governor Road
Hershey, PA 17033

AOT Library
Automotive Organization Team
P.O. Box 1742
Midland, MI 48640

The Archives of Harrah's Automobile Collection
Box 10
Reno, NV 89504

Automobile Reference Collection
The Free Library of Philadelphia
Logan Square
Philadelphia, PA 19103

Automotive Literature Library of the Auburn-
Cord-Duesenberg Museum
P. O. Box 271
Auburn, IN 46706

Chrysler Historical Collection
P. O. Box 1919
Detroit, MI 48228

Crawford Auto-Aviation Museum
Western Reserve Historical Society
10825 East Boulevard
Cleveland, OH 44106

Ford Archives
Edison Institute
20900 Oakwood Boulevard
Dearborn, MI 48121

The National Automotive History Collection
Detroit Public Library
5201 Woodward Avenue
Detroit, MI 48202

Society of Automotive Engineers
4000 Commonwealth Drive
Pittsburgh, Pennsylvania 15016

The reference collections and archives listed above are the best known in the United States. When seeking information, allow plenty of time for an answer. For the adventurous archivist, try local libraries throughout the country. Especially valuable are public libraries located in cities in which automobiles were made. For example, the library in Springfield, Massachusetts, has original correspondence concerning the Duryea Brothers and hard-to-find information on the only American-made Rolls-Royces, among many other tidbits of auto lore.

# Automobile Museums

The world of automobile museums is surprisingly volatile. A small collection will make its debut only to disappear within the next few years. There are, however, old standbys, collections that have endured and continue to attract motoring fans. The list below—following the four most unusual collections—is arranged by state and lists the city and phone number of some of the better-known museums in the country.

## HENRY FORD MUSEUM AND GREENFIELD VILLAGE

The Edison Institute
Dearborn, Michigan 48121
(313) 271-1620 information and reservations
(313) 271-1976 24-hour general information
(800) 835-2246, ext. 218

- Open 9 A.M. to 5 P.M. year-round except Thanksgiving, Christmas, and New Year's days.
- Separate admission for the museum and the village. Each is $8 for adults; $4 for children; children under 5 free; $7 for senior citizens. A two-day (consecutive) admission ticket is $15 for adults; $13 for senior citizens.
- Dining facilities on premises.

Henry Ford designed this complex of houses and halls to "reproduce American life as lived; . . . a better and truer impression can be gained than could be had in a month of reading." Between the indoor Henry Ford Museum and the outdoor Greenfield Village, you'll find 254 acres of outstanding artifacts and activities. Besides housing almost 200 automobiles—including the 1909 Model T Ford that "put the world on wheels," a 1915 Cadillac, a 1937 Cord, Franklin D. Roosevelt's "Sunshine Special," the Lincoln that carried John F. Kennedy on November 22, 1963, and an assortment of racing cars—the museum is home to some of the finest collections of steam engines, farm implements and machines, bicycles, and lighting. During warmer weather, the village offers Model T, steamboat, and steam-train rides as well as a carousel. Narrated carriage tours operate year-round.

## INDIANAPOLIS MOTOR SPEEDWAY HALL OF FAME MUSEUM

4790 West 16th Street
Speedway, IN 46222
(317) 241-2500

- Open 9 A.M. to 5 P.M. year-round except Christmas day.
- Admission is $1 for adults; visitors under 16 are free.
- Motel and dining facilities on premises; golf.

The obvious highlight to this museum is the speedway itself, home of the famous Indy 500 and a landmark that the National Register of Historic Places has listed since 1975. The automobile collection, impressive in its own right, includes twenty-five Indianapolis 500 winners as well as a beautiful display of classic and antique passenger vehicles. The Louis Chevrolet Memorial, adjacent to the museum, provides another bit of automobiliana. When the track is not being used for competition or tests, visitors can take a bus tour of the course for an additional $1.

## AUTOMOTIVE HALL OF FAME

P. O. Box 1727
Midland, Michigan 48641-1727
(517) 631-5760

- Open 9 A.M. to 4 P.M. Monday through Friday. Closed on holidays.
- No admission charge.

This non-profit institution may seem less impressive than other museums at first: it displays only one car and one truck, and it offers no activities. To its credit, however, its presents a history of people, a timeline of achievements and accomplishments that inspire the imagination and make innovation and invention seem possible in our super-technological age. The hall of fame also includes a library brimming with automotive memorabilia.

## ALASKA

Alaska Historical and Transportation Museum
Palmer
(907) 745-4493

## ARKANSAS

Museum of Automobiles
Morrilton
(501) 727-5427

## CALIFORNIA

Briggs Cunningham Automotive Museum
Costa Mesa
(714) 546-7660

Museum of Natural History
Los Angeles
(213) 744-3351

## COLORADO

Colorado Car Museum
Colorado Springs
(303) 685-5996

Forney Transportation Museum
Denver
(303) 433-3643

The Ray Dougherty Collection
Longmont
(303) 776-2520

## FLORIDA

Bellm's Cars and Music of Yesterday
Sarasota
(813) 355-6228

Elliot Museum
Hutchinson Island
(305) 225-1961

Museum of Speed
Daytona Beach
(904) 767-0181

## GEORGIA

Stone Mountain Auto Museum
Stone Mountain
(404) 469-9160

## ILLINOIS

The Bureau County Museum of Antique Automobiles
Princeton
(815) 875-2184

Museum of Science and Industry
Chicago
(312) 684-1414

Volo Sportscars Museum
Volo
(815) 385-3644

## INDIANA

Auburn-Cord-Duesenberg Museum
Auburn
(219) 925-1444

Discovery Hall Museum
South Bend
(219) 284-9714

Early Wheels Museum
Terre Haute
(812) 232-9446

Indiana Transportation Museum
Noblesville
(317) 773-6000

Indianapolis Motor Speedway Hall of Fame Museum
Indianapolis
(317) 241-2500

## MAINE

Owls Head Transportation Museum
Owls Head
(207) 594-4418

Wells Auto Museum
Wells
(207) 646-9064

## MARYLAND

Ordnance Museum
Aberdeen Proving Ground
(301) 278-5201

## MASSACHUSETTS

Museum of Transportation
Jamaica Plain
(617) 522-6140

## MICHIGAN

Automotive Hall of Fame
Midland
(517) 631-5760

Detroit Historical Museum
Detroit
(313) 833-1805

Gilmore Car Museum
Hickory Corners
(616) 671-5089

Henry Ford Museum
Dearborn
(313) 271-1620
(313) 271-1976
(800) 835-2246, ext. 218

Poll Museum of Transportation
Holland
(616) 399-1955

R. E. Olds Museum
Lansing
(517) 372-0422

## MISSOURI

Kelsey's Antique Cars
Camdenton
(314) 346-2506

National Museum of Transport
St. Louis
(314) 965-7998


Patee House Museum
St. Joseph
(816) 232-8206


## MONTANA

Towe Antique Ford Collection
Deer Lodge
(406) 846-3111


## NEBRASKA

The Harold Warp Pioneer Village
Minden
(308) 832-1181


## NEVADA

The William F. Harrah Automobile Foundation
Harrah's Automobile Collection
Reno (Sparks)
(702) 355-3500


## NEW YORK

Automotive Museum
Freeport
(516) 378-6666

# OHIO

Crawford Auto Aviation Museum
Cleveland
(216) 721-5722

# PENNSYLVANIA

Boyertown Vehicle Museum
Boyertown
(215) 367-2090

Pollock Automobile Museum
Pottstown
(215) 323-7108

Swigart Museum
Huntingdon
(814) 643-0885
(814) 643-3000

# SOUTH CAROLINA

Stock Car Hall of Fame/Joe Weatherly Museum
Darlington
(803) 393-2103

# SOUTH DAKOTA

Horseless Carriage Museum
Rapid City
(605) 342-2279

---

Pioneer Auto Museum
Murdo
(605) 669-2691

## TEXAS

Pate Museum of Transportation
Fort Worth
(817) 332-1161

San Antonio Museum of Transportation
San Antonio
(512) 226-5544

## VIRGINIA

Luray Caverns Car and Carriage Caravan
Luray
(703) 743-6552

Roaring Twenties Antique Car Museum
Hood
(703) 948-6290

U.S. Army Transportation Museum
Fort Eustis
(804) 878-3603

## WASHINGTON, D.C.

Smithsonian Institution
(202) 357-2401

## WISCONSIN

Brooks Stevens Automotive Museum
Mequon
(414) 241-4185

Four Wheel Drive Foundation
Clintonville
(715) 823-2141

## WYOMING

Johnson County, Jim Gatchell Memorial Museum
Buffalo
(307) 684-9331

## Harrah's Cars

The Harrah Collection began in 1948, when William F. Harrah acquired a 1911 Maxwell. When Harrah died in 1978, he had more than one thousand vehicles within the collection. Holiday Inns bought Harrah's in 1980 and announced that it would divest itself of the automobiles. A pamphlet from the organization explains that "prominent Nevadans, including state and national governmental officials, appealed to Holiday Inns to reconsider. And in 1982, at the suggestion of Holiday Inns, a public foundation was formed in Reno to accept a donation of more than 300 of the most prized cars in the collection, as chosen by a group of experts. . . . When the donation is complete, it will amount to over $30 million, one of the largest corporate gifts in American business history." The first hundred cars, listed below, were declared gifts to the Harrah Automobile Foundation in 1982.

1906 Adams-Farwell
1937 Airomobile Experimental

1952 Allstate A-230
1933 Auburn 12-161A V12
1933 Austin-American Series 2-75
1924 Brooks Steamer Model 2
1913 Cadillac
1933 Cadillac 425C V16 (Al Jolson's)
1976 Cadillac Eldorado
1917 Chevrolet D-5
1941 Chevrolet Special Design AH
1969 Chevrolet Corvair 500
1941 Chrysler Newport
1956 Chrysler 300B
1965 Citroen 2CV
1972 Continental Mark IV
1936 Cord Experimental Supercharged
1937 Cord 812 Supercharged
1941 Crosley CB41
1919 Cunningham V-3
1901 De Dion-Bouton A No. 2
1937 Detroit Electric 99
1925 Duesenberg A
1903 Duryea 3-Wheeled
1934 Dymaxion Experimental
1961 Fiat 600 D. Model Y
1903 Ford A
1909 Ford T 2 Pedal-2 Lever
1915 Ford T
1926 Ford TT
1931 Ford A
1955 Ford Thunderbird
1903 Franklin
1908 Franklin 145
1917 Franklin 9-A
1930 Franklin 145
1933 Franklin 17-B V12

---

1908 Frayer-Miller B
1951 Frazer Manhattan
1918 Frontmobile
1974 Garlits' Winn's Charger
1961 Ghia L. 6. 4 (Frank Sinatra's)
1937 Hispano-Suiza J12
1921 Holmes Series 4 (Air Cooled)
1929 Hudson Greater Hudson
1911 Hupmobile 20
1914 IMP Z
1926 Jordan Playboy J
1925 Julian
1947 Kaiser K-100 Pinconning Special
1904 Knox Tudor
1955 Kurtis Ansted Rotary Special
1897 Leon Bollee
1927 Lincoln L-134B
1962 Lincoln-Continental 86 (John F. Kennedy's)
1940 Lincoln-Zephyr 06H (Mickey Rooney's)
1899 Locomobile Steam
1965 Lotus-Ford 38
1949 M.G. TC
1911 Maxwell AB (William F. Harrah's original car)
1923 Maxwell Good Maxwell (Jack Benny's)
1925 McFarlan Twin Valve 6-154
1936 Mercedes-Benz 500k
1956 Mercedes-Benz 300SL
1913 Mercer Series J, Type 35
1949 Mercury (James Dean's in *Rebel Without a Cause*)
1913 Metz
1934 Morgan Super Sports J.A.P.
1902 Oldsmobile R Runabout
1910 Oldsmobile Limited
1954 Oldsmobile Super 88
1966 Oldsmobile Toronado

1900 Packard B
1938 Packard 1607 V12 (Harrah's)
1942 Packard Super 8 Custom 180
1892 Panhard & Levassor
1913 Peugeot BeBe
1938 Phantom Corsair Experimental
1913 Pierce-Arrow 66 A-1
1929 Plymouth Q
1911 Pope-Hartford W
1950 Porsche 356
1975 Prudhomme Funny Car
1919 Rolls-Royce Silver Ghost
1923 Rolls-Royce Springfield Silver Ghost
1959 Scimitar
1912 Selden 47-R
1960 Shamrock
1913 Stanley Steam 810
1926 Stanley Steam 262
1910 Stearns 30-60
1924 Studebaker EK Big 6
1913 Stutz B
1907 Thomas 35
1948 Tucker 48
1960 Vespa
1909 White Steam O
1924 Wills-St. Claire B-68
1942 Willys MT-TUG
1899 Winton

# Cars of the Smithsonian

Our national museum has a collection of cars, trucks, and motorcycles that is perhaps the best known in the country. Every year more than 5.3-million people visit the museum. Listed below are the cars of the collection and a brief annotation of why they're important. The museum is open from 10 a.m. to 5:30 p.m. every day but Christmas.

Smith Hempstone Oliver's book *The Smithsonian Collection of Automobiles and Motorcycles* provided the information below. For details on the museum's most current acquisitions, such as a Tom Petty racing car, a Stanley steamer from 1910, or a Ford Model T, contact the National Museum of American History directly.

## DURYEA 1893-94

This car, designed by Charles E. and J. Frank Duryea, is credited as the first operable gasoline-powered motor vehicle in the United States. Water cooled, the automobile is a 1-cylinder, 4-cycle, 4-horsepower vehicle. It first ran in September 1893.

## HAYNES 1894

The car in the museum is now a 2-horsepower auto with pneumatic tires and a "new" steering mechanism. When first built, the car had a 1-horsepower, 2-cycle Sintz engine, wire-spoke wheels, and a swinging front axle. The car made its first working appearance in the streets on Independence Day 1894. Designed by Elwood Haynes, this vehicle is often mistakenly dubbed the first car of America.

## BALZER 1894

This lightweight open vehicle has a 3-cylinder, air-cooled, rotary-type engine. The car stands less than 6 feet long and 3 feet wide, with the front wheels measuring in considerably smaller than the back wheels.

## OLDS 1897

Ransom E. Olds was a pioneer in the auto industry; this vehicle is one of the first five that Olds built and the only one of these originals that still exists. Built in 1897, the car has a 6-horsepower, 1-cylinder, water-cooled engine.

## WINTON 1898

Designed and built by Alexander Winton, the vehicle at the museum is the first car to be sold by the Winton Motor Carriage Company. The engine is 1-cylinder and water-cooled.

## KNOX 1899

This vehicle built by Harry Knox is a good example of an early three-wheeler. Smith Hempstone Oliver, author of a very informative book on the Smithsonian collection, writes, "When it paraded in the Hudson-Fulton celebration in New York in 1909, this car won a prize of $25 for being the oldest machine to cover the line of march under its own power." The engine is 1-cylinder, 8-horsepower, and air-cooled.

## KELSEY AND TILNEY 1899

This experimental car was never produced in quantity. The three-wheeler, built by Carl W. Kelsey and I. Sheldon Tilney, has a 1-cylinder, 8-horsepower, water-cooled engine.

## AUTOCAR 1901

This 2-cylinder, water-cooled automobile is shaft-driven, a feature that was brand new in 1901 in the United States. Louis S. Clarke designed the car.

## PIERCE MOTORETTE 1901

This 3½-horsepower, 1-cylinder, water-cooled automobile was built by the George N. Pierce Company. Pierce Motorettes established a name for themselves when they succeeded in finishing an endurance run from New York to Buffalo. They averaged approximately 12 miles an hour in the 465-mile race.

## FRANKLIN 1902

The museum's Franklin was the first to be sold by the H. H. Franklin Manufacturing Company and the third one to be built. The price at the time was a whopping $1,250 for the 4-cylinder, 7-horsepower, air-cooled car.

## Winton Racing Car 1902

This fabled car, the "Bullet No. 1," raced to a successful finish on a horse-race track in Cleveland, Ohio, averaging approximately 55 miles an hour on the 10-mile track. In 1903 Winton again drove this car in a race; the results were quite impressive. He achieved an average speed of 68.96 miles an hour, driving one mile in just over 52 seconds.

## WINTON RACING CAR 1903

"Bullet No. 2" holds its own place in history as one of the first cars to incorporate an 8-cylinder, in-line engine into its mechanics. Specifically, the car has two 4-cylinder, in-line motors.

## WINTON 1903

Wintons also made a name for themselves as endurance cars; this one made the first transcontinental trip in the United States. It has a 2-cylinder, 4-cycle, water-cooled engine.

## MODEL A CADILLAC 1903

The example in the museum is one of the Cadillac Automobile Company's first year's cars; the cost was $850 for the 1-cylinder, water-cooled vehicle.

## OLDSMOBILE 1903

Smith Hempstone Oliver credits this car as being "one of the most popular of its day." The 1-cylinder car sold for $650 from Olds Motor Works.

## SIMPLEX 1912

This car, No. 778 from the Simplex Automobile Company, was a powerful car for its day and thus drew a following. Although it was rated at 50 horsepower, it could reach 80 miles an hour.

## PIERCE-ARROW 1912

This 36-horsepower car sold for $4,000 from the Pierce-Arrow Motor Car Company. It's 6-cylinder engine was still relatively rare in those days.

## COLUMBIA MARK LX 1904

This electric automobile was manufactured by the Electric Vehicle Company. It was generally considered to be more reliable than a gasoline-powered car.

## ROLLS-ROYCE MODEL 1907

This quarter-scale model does not run. It is a representation of a Silver Ghost that ran a 15,000-mile reliability course; any parts in which wear was detected were replaced at a cost that today would most likely fall below $25. The original car had a 6-cylinder, approximately 48-horsepower engine.

## SEARS MODEL P DELIVERY CAR 1911

A high-wheeler, this motorized wagon used wheels similar to carriage wheels. The 2-cylinder, air-cooled, 14-horsepower vehicle sold for $445 in 1911.

## RAUCH AND LANG 1914

This electric is a good example of the kind of car that was very popular in 1914. The 2½-horsepower enclosed body vehicle was made by the Rauch and Lang Carriage Company.

## DUDGEON STEAM WAGON 1866

Made by Richard Dudgeon of New York City, this vehicle is most likely the oldest self-propelled machine to be built in the U.S.

## FORD 1913

The engine on this Model T is numbered 211098. Far from being a stripped-down model, this car includes a Hoyt ammeter, a Stewart and Clare speedometer, a New Haven clock, running-board toolbox, electric headlights, windshield wiper, antirattling gadgets, a Ward-Leonard electric starting motor and electric generator, and a pedal accelerator. The 4-cylinder, 4-cycle, water-cooled car sold for about $600 without the accessories.

## OLDSMOBILE 1918

Olds Motor Works sold this 4-door, 5-passenger touring car for $1,185 when new. The 6-cylinder, 19-horsepower engine is water-cooled.

## CADILLAC CHASSIS 1923

The chassis, when compared with the Smithsonian's Model A Cadillac of 1903, shows how Cadillac construction changed over a twenty-year period. This is a V-8, water-cooled engine that rates 60 horsepower.

## FRANKLIN 1924

H. H. Franklin Manufacturing Company produced this car, which is considered an anomaly of its day because

---

it retained an air-cooled engine. The 4-door, 5-passenger automobile has a 6-cylinder, approximately 25-horsepower engine.

## EXPERIMENTAL CHRYSLER 1964

This turbine-powered vehicle is No. 45 out of fifty similar experimental cars with 130-horsepower engines. Its performance, however, rates what a 200-horsepower piston engine might. The engine weighs only 410 pounds; its other interesting statistic—it has 80 percent fewer moving parts than an analogous piston engine.

## LOCOMOBILE 1900

F. E. and F. O. Stanley, of the steamers' fame, sold their steam car company to the people who produced Locomobiles. This "Style 2" type car sold on July 4, 1900 for $750.

## MODEL OF THE SELDEN GASOLINE AUTOMOBILE 1879

This model represents an important issue that was raised in the early days of auto history. George Selden was awarded the first patent (No. 549, 160) for an internal-combustion-engine-powered automobile, which was given to him on November 5, 1895. For many years Selden received royalties from other car manufacturers. It wasn't until Henry Ford that someone challenged Selden—and won.

## RIKER APPROXIMATELY 1900

Built by the Riker Motor Vehicle Company, this closed car has an unusual feature—a voice tube that runs from the inside to the outside, where the driver's seat is located.

## WHITE

A 2-cylinder steam car, this vehicle is numbered 260. It was built by the White Sewing Machine Company.

## Major Automobile Clubs

Antique Automobile Club of America
501 W. Governor Road
Hershey, PA 17033

Classic Car Club of America
P. O. Box 443
Madison, NJ 07940

Contemporary Historical Vehicle Association
Box 40
Antioch, TN 37013

Horseless Carriage Club of America
Box 1000
312 E. Las Tunas Drive
San Gabriel, CA 91776

Mid-America Old Time Automobile Association
920 Eisenhower Street
Tupelo, MS 38801

Milestone Car Society
R.D. 334
7702 E Street
Zionsville, IN 46077

The Society of Automotive Historians
2105 Stackhouse Drive
Yardley, PA 19067

Steam Automobile Club of America, Inc.
1937 E. 71st Street
Chicago, IL 60649

The Veteran Motor Car Club of America
105 Elm Street
Andover, MA 01810

The Vintage Sports Car Club
2035 Greenwood
Wilmette, IL 60091

Vintage Sports Car Club of America
170 Wetherill Road
Garden City, NY 11570

## Classic Car Club of America
## American Classics

The Classic Car Club of America, originally a small group of auto enthusiasts, is now an international organization with a membership growing toward 5,000.

Among its many activities are the Grand Classic, in which cars are rated on the expertise and quality of restoration, and the Classic CARavan, a 120-car tour that draws from the U.S. and Canadian membership roster. Listed below are the distinctive American automobile makes or models (from 1925 through 1948—the "Classic" era), that have earned classic status. For more information, write to the Classic Car Club of America, P. O. Box 443, Madison, NJ 07940

### A.C.
### Adler*
### Amilcar*—Supercharged Sports Model
### Auburn—All 8- and 12-cylinder
### Blackhawk
### Brewster*—All Heart Front Fords
### Brough Superior*
### Buick—1931–1942 90 Series   Custom bodied*
### Cadillac—All 1925 through 1935   All 12s and
16s   1938–1941—60 Special   1936–1948—All 67, 70, 72, 75, 80, 85, 90 Custom bodied*
### Chrysler—1926 through 1930 Imperial 80   1931 through 1936 Imperial series CG, CH, CL, and CW   Also Newports and Thunderbolts   Custom bodied*
### Cord
### Cunningham
### Dagmar—25–70 Model only
### Doble
### Dorris
### Duesenberg
### duPont
### Franklin—Except 1933–1934 Olympic Sixes
### Frazer Nash*
### Graham Paige—Custom bodied*
### Hispano Suiza

---

**Hudson**—1929 Series L   Custom bodied*
**Jordan**—Speedway Series 'Z'
**Julian***
**Kissel**—1925–1926   1927—8–75   1928—8–90 and 8–90
White Eagle   1929–1930—8–125
**LaSalle**—1927 through 1933
**Lincoln**—All L, KA, KB, and K   1941—168 H 1942—268
H
**Lincoln Continental**
**Locomobile**—All models 48 and 90   1927–1929—8–30
**Marmon**—All 16-cylinder   1925–1926—74   1927—
75 1928—E75   1930—Big 8   1931—88 and Big 8
**McFarlan**
**Mercer**
**Minerva**—Except 4-cylinder cars
**Moon**—Custom bodied*
**Nash**—1930—Twin Ignition 8*   1931—Series 890*
1932—Series 990, Advanced 8, and Ambassador 8*
1933 and 1934—Ambassador 8*
**Packard**—All sixes and eights 1925 through 1934   All
12-cylinder models   1935—Models 1200 through
1205, 1207 and 1208   1936—Models 1400 through 1405,
1407 and 1408   1937—Models 1500 through 1502
and 1506 through 1508   1938—Models 1603 through
1605, 1607 and 1608   1939—Models 1703, 1705,
1707, and 1708   1940—Models 1803, 1804, 1805, 1806,
1807, and 1808   1941—Models 1903, 1904, 1905,
1906, 1907, and 1908   1942—Models 2003, 2004, 2005,
and 2006, 2007, and 2008   1946 and 1947—Models
2106 and 2126 All Darrin-bodied   Custom bodied*
**Peerless**—1926—28, Series 69   1930–1931—Custom 8
1932—Deluxe Custom 8
**Pierce-Arrow**
**Reo**—1931 through 1933—8–31, 8–35, 8–52, Royale
Custom 8   1934—N1, N2, and 8-52

---

**Revere**
**Roamer**—1925—8–88, 6-54e, and 4-75   1926—4-75e and
8-88   All 1927 and 1928   1929—8-88 and 8-125
1930—8-125
**Rolls-Royce**
**Ruxton**
**Squire**
**Stearns-Knight**
**Stevens-Duryea**
**Studebaker**—1929–1933, President Series
**Stutz**
**Talbot**—105C 110C
**Talbot Lago**—150C
**Wills-St. Claire**
**Willys-Knight**—Series 66*

*Please apply for further details.

# The Most Collectible American Cars

The following list includes only the uppermost echelon,
the crème de la crème of all collectible American cars
of the period. These cars are expected to rise in value
faster than other collectible American cars and are
therefore considered to be the collector's best choices in
terms of financial investment.

# THE MOST COLLECTIBLE AMERICAN CARS OF THE 1940S (POST WWII)

| YEAR | MAKE | ORIGINAL PRICE | NUMBER PRO-DUCED | APPROXIMATE NUMBER STILL EXISTING |
|---|---|---|---|---|
| 1946 | Chrysler Town and Country Convertible | $2743 | 2789 | 8 |
| 1946 | Chrysler Town and Country Two-Door Hardtop | $2743 | 7 | 1 |
| 1946 | Ford Super Deluxe Sportsman Convertible | $2041 | 723 | 20 |
| 1946 | Ford Super Deluxe Station Wagon | $1500 | 16,960 | 17 |
| 1946 | Lincoln Continental Cabriolet | $4476 | 201 | 20 |
| 1946 | Lincoln Continental Coupe | $4392 | 265 | 26 |
| 1946 | Lincoln Convertible Coupe | $2883 | unknown | unknown |
| 1946 | Mercury Sportsman Convertible Coupe | $2263 | 205 | 3 |
| 1947 | Chrysler Town and Country Convertible | $2889 | 2789 | 10 |
| 1947 | Ford Super Deluxe Station Wagon | $1617 | 16,104 | 20 |
| 1947 | Ford Super Deluxe Convertible | $2041 | 2774 | 78 |
| 1947 | Lincoln Continental Cabriolet | $4476 | 738 | 73 |
| 1947 | Lincoln Continental Coupe | $4392 | 831 | 80 |

**YOU AND THE WORLD OF CARS**

# THE MOST COLLECTIBLE AMERICAN CARS OF THE
## 1940S (POST WWII) (*Continued*)

| YEAR | MAKE | ORIGINAL PRICE | NUMBER PRO- DUCED | APPROXIMATE NUMBER STILL EXISTING |
|------|------|----------------|-------------------|-----------------------------------|
| 1947 | Lincoln Convertible Coupe | $2883 | unknown | unknown |
| 1948 | Chrysler Town and Country Convertible | $3420 | 2789 | 27 |
| 1948 | Ford Super Deluxe Sportsman Convertible | $2282 | 28 | 1 |
| 1948 | Ford Super Deluxe Station Wagon | $1700 | 8912 | 20 |
| 1948 | Lincoln Continental Cabriolet | $4746 | 452 | 45 |
| 1948 | Lincoln Convertible Coupe | $2900 | unknown | unknown |
| 1948 | Tucker | $2495– $5000 | 51 | 48 |
| 1949 | Buick Super Estate Station Wagon | $3178 | 1847 | 3 |
| 1949 | Chrysler Town and Country Convertible | $3995 | 1000 | 20 |
| 1949 | Mercury Convertible | $2400 | 16,765 | 12 |

(Source: *The Investor's Illustrated Guide to American Convertible and Special-Interest Automobiles, 1946–1976*, by Charles Webb)

# THE MOST COLLECTIBLE AMERICAN CARS OF THE 1950S

| YEAR | MAKE | ORIGINAL PRICE | NUMBER PRODUCED | APPROXIMATE NUMBER STILL EXISTING |
|------|------|---------|----------|----------|
| 1950 | Chrysler Town and Country Newport | $4003 | 700 | 20 |
| 1950 | Mercury Convertible | $2410 | 8341 | 17 |
| 1950 | Oldsmobile 88 Convertible | $2294 | 9127 | 20 |
| 1951 | Ford Custom Station Wagon | $2107 | 29,017 | 12 |
| 1951 | Hudson Hornet Six Convertible Brougham | $3019 | 43,666 | 129 |
| 1951 | Mercury Convertible | $2412 | 6759 | 14 |
| 1951 | Nash Healey Convertible | $4063 | 104 | 10 |
| 1952 | Hudson Hornet Six Convertible Brougham | $3318 | 35,921 | 45 |
| 1952 | Nash Healey Convertible | $5000 | 150 | 15 |
| 1953 | Buick Skylark Convertible | $5500 | 1690 | 40 |
| 1953 | Cadillac Eldorado Convertible | $7750 | 532 | 33 |
| 1953 | Chevrolet Corvette Convertible | $3513 | 300 | 15 |
| 1953 | Hudson Hornet Convertible Brougham | $3342 | 24,833 | 26 |

**YOU AND THE WORLD OF CARS**

# THE MOST COLLECTIBLE AMERICAN CARS OF THE
## 1950S (Continued)

| YEAR | MAKE | ORIGINAL PRICE | NUMBER PRO-DUCED | APPROXIMATE NUMBER STILL EXISTING |
|------|------|------|------|------|
| 1953 | Nash Healey Le Mans Hardtop | $5000 | 162 | 16 |
| 1953½ | Oldsmobile 98 Fiesta Convertible | $5715 | 458 | 29 |
| 1953 | Packard Caribbean Convertible | $5210 | 750 | 50 |
| 1954 | Buick Skylark Convertible | $4483 | 836 | 20 |
| 1954 | Chevrolet Corvette Convertible | $3523 | 3640 | 90 |
| 1954 | Kaiser Darrin Roadster | $3668 | 435 | 230 |
| 1954 | Nash Healey Convertible | $5000 | 90 | 9 |
| 1954 | Nash Healey Le Mans Hardtop | $5128 | 90 | 9 |
| 1954 | Packard Caribbean Convertible | $6100 | 400 | 40 |
| 1955 | Chevrolet Bel Air Nomad Station Wagon | $2571 | 8386 | 1250 |
| 1955 | Chevrolet Bel Air Sport Coupe | $2166 | 185,562 | 3525 |
| 1955 | Chevrolet Corvette Convertible | $2934 | 700 | 25 |
| 1955 | Chevrolet 210 Sport Coupe | $2000 | 11,675 | 221 |

| YEAR | MAKE | ORIGINAL PRICE | NUMBER PRO-DUCED | APPROXIMATE NUMBER STILL EXISTING |
|---|---|---|---|---|
| 1955 | Chrysler 300 Coupe | $4055 | 1725 | 25 |
| 1955 | Ford Fairlane Crown Victoria Skyliner | $2272 | 1999 | 17 |
| 1955 | Ford Fairlane Sunliner Convertible | $2204 | 49,966 | 284 |
| 1955 | Ford Thunderbird Convertible | $2695 | 16,155 | 1600 |
| 1955 | Kurtis 500 M Sports Car | $5000 | 24 | 12 |
| 1955 | Packard Caribbean Convertible | $5932 | 500 | 50 |
| 1955 | Pontiac Star Chief Custom Safari Station Wagon | $2714 | 3760 | 32 |
| 1956 | Chevrolet Bel Air Convertible | $2409 | 41,268 | 850 |
| 1956 | Chevrolet Bel Air Nomad Station Wagon | $2673 | 7886 | 1100 |
| 1956 | Chevrolet Bel Air Sport Coupe | $2142 | 128,382 | 2560 |
| 1956 | Chevrolet Corvette Convertible | $3120 | 3467 | 110 |
| 1956 | Chevrolet Sport Coupe | $2029 | 18616 | 370 |
| 1956 | Chrysler 300-B Coupe | $4312 | 1102 | 17 |
| 1956 | Continental Mark II Hardtop | $9538 | 2550 | 1200 |

# THE MOST COLLECTIBLE AMERICAN CARS OF THE
## 1950S (*Continued*)

| YEAR | MAKE | ORIGINAL PRICE | NUMBER PRO-DUCED | APPROXIMATE NUMBER STILL EXISTING |
|------|------|----------------|------------------|-----------------------------------|
| 1956 | Ford Fairlane Crown Victoria Skyliner | $2164 | 603 | 8 |
| 1956 | Ford Fairlane Sunliner Convertible | $2212 | 58,147 | 497 |
| 1956 | Ford Thunderbird Convertible | $2842 | 15,631 | 1500 |
| 1956 | Lincoln Premier Convertible | $4318 | 2447 | 35 |
| 1956 | Packard Caribbean Convertible | $5992 | 276 | 30 |
| 1956 | Packard Caribbean Hardtop | $5495 | 263 | 25 |
| 1956 | Pontiac Star Chief Custom Safari Station Wagon | $2831 | 4042 | 30 |
| 1957 | Cadillac Eldorado Brougham | $13,074 | 400 | 240 |
| 1957 | Chevrolet Bel Air Convertible | $2611 | 47,562 | 1400 |
| 1957 | Chevrolet Bel Air Nomad Station Wagon | $2857 | 6103 | 1250 |
| 1957 | Chevrolet Bel Air Sport Coupe | $2399 | 166,426 | 5000 |
| 1957 | Chevrolet Corvette Convertible | $3465 | 6339 | 300 |

| YEAR | MAKE | ORIGINAL PRICE | NUMBER PRO-DUCED | APPROXIMATE NUMBER STILL EXISTING |
|------|------|----------------|------------------|-----------------------------------|
| 1957 | Chevrolet 210 Sport Coupe | $2304 | 22631 | 700 |
| 1957 | Chrysler 300-C Convertible | $5294 | 484 | 6 |
| 1957 | Continental Mark II Convertible | $10,000 | 2 | 2 |
| 1957 | Continental Mark II Hardtop | $9620 | 454 | 260 |
| 1957 | Ford Fairlane 500 Skyliner Retractable Hardtop | $2945 | 20766 | 250 |
| 1957 | Ford Fairlane 500 Sunliner Convertible | $2389 | 77,728 | 592 |
| 1957 | Ford Thunderbird Convertible | $3088 | 21,380 | 2100 |
| 1957 | Pontiac Bonneville Convertible | $5782 | 630 | 20 |
| 1957 | Pontiac Star Chief Custom Safari Station Wagon | $2900 | 1292 | 20 |
| 1958 | Cadillac Eldorado Brougham | $13,074 | 304 | 182 |
| 1958 | Chevrolet Bel Air Impala Convertible | $2841 | 55,989 | 690 |
| 1958 | Chevrolet Bel Air Impala Sport Coupe | $2693 | 125,480 | 1549 |
| 1958 | Chevrolet Corvette Convertible | $3631 | 9168 | 160 |
| 1958 | Chrysler 300-D Convertible | $5538 | 191 | 4 |

# THE MOST COLLECTIBLE AMERICAN CARS OF THE
## 1950S *(Continued)*

| YEAR | MAKE | ORIGINAL PRICE | NUMBER PRO-DUCED | APPROXIMATE NUMBER STILL EXISTING |
|------|------|----------------|------------------|-----------------------------------|
| 1958 | Chrysler 300-D Coupe | $5108 | 618 | 10 |
| 1958 | DeSoto Adventurer Convertible | $4314 | unknown | unknown |
| 1958 | Ford Fairlane 500 Skyliner Retractable Hardtop | $3138 | 14,713 | 166 |
| 1959 | Chevrolet Corvette Convertible | $3875 | 9670 | 200 |
| 1959 | Chrysler 300-E Convertible | $5659 | 140 | 5 |
| 1959 | Ford Galaxie Sky-liner Retractable Hardtop | $3346 | 12,915 | 310 |

(Source: *The Investor's Illustrated Guide to American Convertible and Special-Interest Automobiles, 1946–1976,* by Charles Webb)

# THE MOST COLLECTIBLE AMERICAN CARS OF THE 1960S

| YEAR | MAKE | ORIGINAL PRICE | NUMBER PRO-DUCED | APPROXIMATE NUMBER STILL EXISTING |
|------|------|----------------|------------------|-----------------------------------|
| 1960 | Chevrolet Corvette Convertible | $3872 | 10,261 | 300 |
| 1960 | Chrysler 300-F Convertible | $5766 | 248 | 7 |
| 1960 | Chrysler 300-F Coupe | $5336 | 964 | 26 |
| 1961 | Chevrolet Corvette Convertible | $3934 | 10,939 | 387 |
| 1961 | Chrysler 300-G Convertible | $5841 | 337 | 8 |
| 1961 | Lincoln Continental Convertible | $6713 | 2857 | 250 |
| 1962 | Chevrolet Corvette Convertible | $3026 | 75,719 | 5040 |
| 1962 | Ford Thunderbird Sports Roadster | $5439 | 1427 | 140 |
| 1962 | Lincoln Continental Convertible | $6720 | 3212 | 312 |
| 1963 | Buick Riviera Sport Coupe | $4333 | 40,000 | 1686 |
| 1963 | Chevrolet Corvette Stingray Convertible | $4037 | 10,919 | 1020 |
| 1963 | Chevrolet Corvette Stingray Sport Coupe | $4252 | 10,594 | 1008 |
| 1963 | Ford Thunderbird Sports Roadster | $5563 | 455 | 50 |
| 1963 | Lincoln Continental Convertible | $6916 | 3138 | 300 |

**YOU AND THE WORLD OF CARS**

# THE MOST COLLECTIBLE AMERICAN CARS OF THE
## 1960S *(Continued)*

| YEAR | MAKE | ORIGINAL PRICE | NUMBER PRODUCED | APPROXIMATE NUMBER STILL EXISTING |
|---|---|---|---|---|
| 1963 | Studebaker Avanti | $4445 | 3744 | 1500 |
| 1964 | Chevrolet Corvette Stingray Convertible | $4037 | 13,925 | 1531 |
| 1964 | Chevrolet Corvette Stingray Sport Coupe | $4252 | 8304 | 1500 |
| 1964½ | Ford Mustang Convertible | $2600 | 28,833 | 2306 |
| 1964½ | Ford Mustang Two-door Hardtop | $2300 | 92,705 | 7416 |
| 1964 | Lincoln Continental Convertible | $6916 | 3328 | 400 |
| 1964 | Studebaker Avanti | $4445 | 795 | 350 |
| 1965 | Chevrolet Chevelle Malibu Super Sport Convertible | $2750 | 19,765 | 2769 |
| 1965 | Chevrolet Corvette Stingray Convertible | $4106 | 15,376 | 2152 |
| 1965 | Chevrolet Corvette Stingray Sport Coupe | $4321 | 8186 | 1600 |
| 1965 | Ford Mustang Convertible | $2614 | 73,112 | 7896 |
| 1965 | Lincoln Continental Convertible | $6938 | 3356 | 466 |
| 1965 | Shelby American GT 350 Fastback | $4400 | 550 | 59 |
| 1966 | Chevrolet Corvette Stingray Convertible | $4084 | 17,762 | 3730 |

| YEAR | MAKE | ORIGINAL PRICE | NUMBER PRODUCED | APPROXIMATE NUMBER STILL EXISTING |
|------|------|------|------|------|
| 1966 | Chevrolet Corvette Stingray Sport Coupe | $4295 | 9958 | 2000 |
| 1966 | Ford Mustang Convertible | $2653 | 72,119 | 11,899 |
| 1966 | Lincoln Continental Convertible | $6383 | 3180 | 588 |
| 1966 | Oldsmobile Tornado | $4617 | 40,963 | unknown |
| 1966 | Shelby American GT 350 Fastback | $4428 | 2378 | 392 |
| 1967 | Chevrolet Camaro Super Sport Convertible | $2704 | 220,900 | 66270 |
| 1967 | Chevrolet Corvette Stingray Convertible | $4141 | 14,436 | 4330 |
| 1967 | Chevrolet Corvette Stingray Sport Coupe | $4353 | 8504 | 3000 |
| 1967 | Pontiac Firebird Convertible | $2903 | 15,582 | 3583 |
| 1968 | Chevrolet Camaro Convertible | $2908 | 235,100 | 88,397 |
| 1968 | Chevrolet Camaro Sport Coupe | $2694 | 235,100 | 88,397 |
| 1968 | Chevrolet Corvette Stingray Convertible | $4420 | 16,608 | 8304 |
| 1968 | Pontiac Firebird Convertible | $3019 | 16,960 | 5936 |
| 1968½ | Rambler AMX Sport Coupe | $3245 | 6725 | 2360 |

# THE MOST COLLECTIBLE AMERICAN CARS OF THE
## 1960S *(continued)*

| YEAR | MAKE | ORIGINAL PRICE | NUMBER PRO-DUCED | APPROXIMATE NUMBER STILL EXISTING |
|------|------|----------------|------------------|-----------------------------------|
| 1968 | Shelby American Cobra GT 500 Convertible | $5000 | 574 | 206 |
| 1968 | Shelby American Cobra GT 350 Convertible | $4500 | 550 | 197 |
| 1969 | Chevrolet Camaro Convertible | $2835 | 243,100 | 121,550 |
| 1969 | Chevrolet Camaro Sport Coupe | $2621 | 243,100 | 121,500 |
| 1969 | Chevrolet Corvette Stingray Convertible | $4420 | 16,608 | 8304 |
| 1969 | Dodge Charger 500 Daytona | $3900 | 505 | 252 |
| 1969 | Pontiac Firebird Convertible | $3028 | 11,649 | 5358 |
| 1969 | Rambler AMX Sport Coupe | $3297 | 8293 | 3706 |
| 1969 | Shelby American GT 500 Convertible | $6300 | 335 | 151 |
| 1969 | Shelby American GT 350 Convertible | $6000 | 194 | 87 |

(Source: *The Investor's Illustrated Guide to American Convertible and Special-Interest Automobiles, 1946–1976,* by Charles Webb)

# THE MOST COLLECTIBLE AMERICAN CARS OF THE 1970S

| YEAR | MAKE | ORIGINAL PRICE | NUMBER PRO-DUCED | APPROXIMATE NUMBER STILL EXISTING |
|------|------|------|------|------|
| 1970 | AMX Sport Coupe | $3395 | 4116 | 2210 |
| 1970 | Chevrolet Corvette Stingray Convertible | $4848 | 6648 | 4188 |
| 1970 | Plymouth Road Runner Superbird | $4298 | 1873 | 1123 |
| 1970 | Shelby American GT 500 Convertible | $6300 | unknown | unknown |
| 1970 | Shelby American GT 350 Convertible | $6000 | unknown | unknown |
| 1971 | Chevrolet Corvette Stingray Convertible | $5299 | 7121 | 5347 |
| 1972 | Chevrolet Corvette Stingray Convertible | $5246 | 6508 | 5323 |
| 1973 | Chevrolet Corvette Stingray Convertible | $5399 | NA | NA |
| 1974 | Chevrolet Corvette Stingray Convertible | $5864 | NA | NA |
| 1975 | Chevrolet Corvette Stingray Convertible | $6537 | NA | NA |

(Source: *The Investor's Illustrated Guide to American Convertible and Special-Interest Automobiles, 1946–1976*, by Charles Webb)

# Special Clubs

And you didn't think there was a club for your car! The list below is a random selection of the numerous automobile clubs currently operating in the United States. Many of these clubs offer helpful information about histories, restorations, and repairs of the cars in question. For an updated list, consult the *Encyclopedia of Associations*, a reference book found in most libraries.

Amphibious Auto Club of America
Auburn-Cord-Duesenberg Club
Buick Compact Club
Classic Thunderbird Club International
Davis 3-Wheel Club of America
De Lorean Club International
Fabulous Fifties Ford Club of America
57 Oldsmobile Chapter
GTO Association of America
Hudson-Essex-Terraplane Club
International Camaro Club
Jordan Register
Kissel Kar Klub
Late Great Chevrolet Association
Lincoln Continental Owners Club
Model "A" Restorers Club
Morgan ¾ Group
National Nostalgic Nova

National Woodie Club
Plymouth Four and Six Cylinder Owners Club
Rickenbacker Car Club
Sunbeam Alpine Club
Super Chevys Limited
Trans Am Club U.S.A.
Winged Warriors

# A Chronology of Early Automobile Journals

1895–1918  *The Horseless Age*
1895–1900  *Motocycle*
1896–1940  *Cycle Trade Journal* (became *Cycle and Automobile Trade Journal* in 1900 and *Automobile Trade Journal* in 1912)
1899–1917  *Automobile* (became *Automotive Industries*)
1899–1902  *Motor Vehicle Review* (merged with *Automobile*)
1899–1907  *Automobile Magazine* (merged with *Automobile*)
1899–present  *Motor Age* (became *Chilton's Motor Age* in 1943)
1900–1940  *Motor World*
1900–1949  *Automobile Topics*
1903–present  *Motor*

# Automobile Reading

Thinking of subscribing to an automobile magazine, but you're not sure which one? A task awaits you. Below are the major car journals listed in *Magazine Marketplace* (1985) and the years in which they were first published.

*AAA World* 1981
*Adventure Road* 1964
*Antique Automobile* 1935
*Antique Motor News* 1961
*ATV News* 1981
*Auto Merchandising News* 1971
*Auto Racing Digest* 1973
*Automobile Quarterly* 1962
*Automotive Age* 1966
*Automotive Body Repair News* 1962
*Automotive Fleet* 1961
*Automotive Industries* 1895
*Automotive Messenger* 1956
*Automotive News* 1925
*Brake and Front End* 1931
*Car & Driver* 1955
*Car Collector & Car Classics* 1978
*Car Craft* 1953
*Car Exchange* 1979
*Cars & Parts* 1957

Chilton's Automotive Marketing   1971
Ford Times   1908
Four Wheeler   1962
Hemmings Motor News   1953
Home & Away Connecticut   1983
Hot Rod Magazine   1948
Mechanics Illustrated   1928
Midwest Motorist   1972
Motor   1903
Motor Age   1899
Motor Service   1921
Motor Trend   1949
Motorland   1917
National Motorist   1924
Off-Road   1969
On Track   1981
Petersen's 4-wheel and Off-Road   1977
Pickup, Van & 4WD   1972
Popular Hot Rodding Magazine   1962
Racing Pictorial   1959
Road and Track   1947
Small World   1962
Special Interest Autos   1970
Street Rodder   1972
Super Chevy   1973
Super Stock & Drag Illustrated   1966
Ward's Auto World   1965

**YOU AND THE WORLD OF CARS**

# Higher Education Behind the Wheel

Most of us think of ourselves as pretty darned good drivers. Trouble is, most of us haven't had the formal training necessary to accurately judge how good we are, and because we haven't had the training, most of us aren't really very good.

But there is hope for those who would like to bring their driving skills and awareness into higher echelons. Enroll in one of the country's professional driving schools. These institutes will teach you basics such as proper seating position and use of the controls, as well as how to correctly understeer (front-wheel skid), oversteer (rear-wheel skid), how to shift, corner, brake, and make emergency maneuvers. Once past these steps, you can go on to classes such as High Performance Driving, Advanced Road Racing, and Championship Competition. If you don't end up in the Indy 500 winner's circle, you will at least get an idea of how the big boys do it.

The five Major American Professional Driving Schools listed below all offer a variety of courses that last from a few hours to five days, and cost anywhere from $100 to $2000. All schools provide cars to learn in, and two of the schools will allow you to use your own.

---

| SCHOOL AND LOCATION | COURSES OFFERED | LENGTH IN DAYS | CARS USED |
|---|---|---|---|
| Skip Barber Racing School<br>Route 7<br>Canaan, Conn.<br>(203) 824-0771 | Competition<br>Adv. Racing<br>Intro. to<br>  Racing<br>Race Weekend<br>Practice Day | 5 or 3<br>2<br><br>1<br>2<br>1 | Formula Fords<br>" "<br>" "<br>" "<br>" "<br>" " |
| Year-round in Conn.,<br>Ohio, Wis., Ind.,<br>Fla., Pa. and<br>other states | | | |
| Bob Bondurant School<br>of High Performance<br>Driving<br>Sears Point<br>International Raceway<br>Highways 37 and 121<br>Sonoma, Calif.<br>(707) 938-4741 | Competition<br>  Road Racing<br>Adv. Road Rac-<br>  ing<br>High Perform-<br>  ance Driving<br>Adv. Highway<br>  Driving | <br>4<br><br>3 or 2<br><br>3 or 2<br><br>1 | Formula Fords<br>  and Mustangs<br>Formula<br>  Fords and<br>  Mustangs<br>Ford Mustangs or<br>  Your Car<br>Ford Escorts or<br>  Your Car |
| Year-round | | | |
| Bertil Roos School of<br>Motor Racing<br>Box 221<br>Blakeslee, Pa.<br>(717) 646-7227 | Competition<br>Highway<br>  Driving<br>Adv. Competition<br>Intro. to Racing | 3<br><br>2<br>1<br>1 | Volvos, Formulas<br>Saab Slide<br>  Cars, Volvos<br>Saab Slide Cars<br>Saab Slide Cars,<br>  Super Fords |
| Apr. to Oct. | | | |
| Jim Russell British<br>School of Motor Racing<br>22255 Eucalyptus Ave.<br>Riverside, Calif.<br>(408) 372-7223 | Competition<br>Championship<br>Race Weekend<br>Adv. Lapping<br>  Days | 3<br>4<br>2<br><br>2 | Formula Fords<br>Formula Russells<br>Formula Russells<br>Formula Russells |
| Year-round in Calif.<br>June to Nov. in N.C. | | | |
| Bill Scott Racing<br>School<br>Box 190<br>Summit Point, W. Va.<br>(304) 725-6512 | Adv. Competition<br>Highway Safety<br>Solo I<br>Friday at the<br>  Track | 1<br>1<br>2 or 1<br><br>1 | Your car<br>Police Malibus<br>Your car<br><br>Your car |
| Feb. to Nov. | | | |

**YOU AND THE WORLD OF CARS**

# America's Ten Most Frightening Places to Drive

Where are the worst places to drive a car in America? The scariest, most confusing spots, with the worst engineering traps and the worst drivers? These are the questions *Popular Mechanics* magazine asked of over 100 experts and cross-country drivers in 1984. The following list, published in the April 1984 issue of the magazine, is what they came up with.

1. Hartford, Conn.—at the junction of I-84 and I-91
2. New York City—the Cross-Bronx Expressway
3. Boston—Route 128 and I-93, equally
4. Dallas—all of the city's expressways
5. Los Angeles—entire freeway system
6. Philadelphia—Schuylkill Expressway, a.k.a. the "Surekill"
7. Baltimore—drunk drivers seem to be a big problem
8. Chicago—the stretch combining I-90 and I-94 called the Dan Ryan Expressway, a.k.a. "Dirty Dan." Also, Edens Expressway (I-94 Extension).
9. Houston—generally inadequate road system
10. Washington, D.C.—The Beltway (I-495)

# America's Ten Most Dangerous Cities to Drive In

According to the National Safety Council, the following are America's 10 most deadly cities to drive in as of 1984. The list is based on the number of auto accident fatalities per 10,000 cars.

1. Houston (4.8 deaths per 10,000 cars)
2. San Antonio, Tex. (4.3)
3. El Paso, Tex. (3.8)
4. Oklahoma City (3.7)
5. Jacksonville, Fla. (3.6)
6. Dallas (3.6)
7. Kansas City, Mo. (3.5)
8. Corpus Christi, Tex. (3.5)
9. Boston (3.1)
10. Nashville (3.0)

# America's Safest

In 1984, the National Safety Council rated these big cities America's safest for driving, based on the number of deaths per 10,000 cars.

1. Minneapolis (0.5 deaths per 10,000 autos)
2. Washington, D.C. (1.0—as rated within the city, not counting the infamous Beltway, which lies outside city limits.)
3. Oakland, Calif. (1.1)
4. St. Paul, Minn. (1.1)
5. Akron, Ohio (1.2)
6. Indianapolis (1.2)
7. Milwaukee (1.2)
8. Buffalo (1.2)
9. Seattle (1.2)
10. Anchorage (1.2)

## The Cadillac Ranch

Travel west along Route 66, just down the road from Amarillo, Texas, and a strange sight might come before you. It's not a mirage; it's not a hallucination. It *is* ten Cadillacs, fins up, buried in the sand, all in a row. These nose-down Caddies are firmly cemented in place. What's up besides the fins, you may ask. Well, it's a sculpture of sorts, commissioned by Stanley Marsh III, a prominent name in Texas. The artists are car buffs Doug Michels, Chip Lord, and Hudson Marquez. Happy trails looking for this one!

# Five Steps Toward the Ideal of Troublefree Driving

The United States Automotive Information Council surveyed professional mechanics in 1984 to find their opinion of the most critical maintenance jobs for keeping an auto in top running condition. Regular attention to these five steps, say the experts, will go far toward making your car a more reliable road machine.

1. Oil and filter changes—the most important and most neglected area of maintenance. Change engine oil and oil filter at least at the intervals recommended in your manual.
2. Tuneups—have the engine checked and tuned at least once a year.
3. Accessory belts—check frequently for cuts, fraying, excessive wear, and replace any that are suspect.
4. Hoses—replace any that are cracked, leaking, oil soaked, spongy feeling, or excessively hard.
5. Suspension and steering lubrication—renew grease at least once a year.

# Eleven Commandments of Car Care

For National Car Month (October) of 1984, the Automobile Club of Southern California issued this list of 11 rules for a healthier automobile:

1. Check oil level every other time you buy gasoline. If it's low, add oil. Consult your owner's manual for recommended oil-change frequency.
2. Check radiator fluid level weekly but *never* when the engine is hot. Add fluid if necessary. Replace antifreeze/coolant solution at least once a year.
3. Check tire pressure weekly. Keep inflated to recommended pressure. Inspect tires monthly for cuts and excessive tread wear. Replace if worn.
4. Check brake fluid monthly. Fill if low. Test brake pedal to be sure it's firm and high.
5. Inspect drive belts, hoses, and clamps monthly. Tighten/replace as needed.
6. Check the battery level and cables weekly. Old-model batteries require water; newer ones show condition by a color indicator. Make sure cables are free of corrosion and are firmly attached.
7. Check air filter monthly. Replace if dirty.
8. Check transmission fluid level monthly.
9. Check windshield wiper solvent and blades monthly. Refill/replace if necessary.

10. Test lights monthly. Turn on ignition and check front, rear, brake, park, low and high beams, and turn indicators. Replace burned-out bulbs and fuses.
11. Adjust your seat belt to fit you snugly before every trip. A belted driver in a well-maintained car is the fundamental commandment for a lifetime of safe driving.

# Index

---